curious
questions

curious
questions

Max Cryer

HarperCollins*Publishers*

First published 2001
Reprinted 2001 (four times), 2002

HarperCollins*Publishers (New Zealand) Limited*
P.O. Box 1, Auckland

ISBN 1 86950 382 1

Set in Janson Text
Designed and typeset by Janine Brougham
Printed by Griffin Press, Australia on 79 gsm Bulky Paperback

Preface

I began hosting 'Curious Questions' on National Radio in 1997 and rapidly discovered that thousands of people were as interested in the English language as I am. Mail has been pouring in ever since — mainly asking about common everyday expressions which everyone knows, but sometimes seeking background about phrases confined to the use of one family connection (usually a non-New Zealander). These are harder, requiring a search through arcane dictionaries of Scottish or Irish dialect and even then sometimes no absolutely neat solution can be found.

There have also been moments of confusion with people who 'thought' an expression or word was derived from a certain source, only to be told it is actually from somewhere else. Scholars who have worked on the background to some phrases in very common use have found as many as ten different possible origins. Each of these is firmly believed by one group of people who vehemently deny the validity of the other nine versions. A good example is OK, the 'origin' of which can be found in five different languages.

These, I have firmly avoided, because it is a rule of human nature that people tend to believe that which they were told first. Sometimes, after a thoroughly researched and annotated account of something has been given, I receive a bunch of letters which begin 'I always thought . . .' or 'My grandmother said . . .' There is no way out of this. Sometimes grandma had the wrong end of the stick, and finding this out can be discomforting.

This book is a selection from some of the hundreds of questions I've received and have tried to answer as completely as possible.

Thanks to Sharon Crosbie, CEO of Radio New Zealand, the organisation that was responsible for getting the ball rolling in the first place.

Max Cryer
June 2001

Why is *AD*, *Anno Domini*, in Latin, but *BC*, meaning *Before Christ*, in English?

There is no clear answer to this. The only clue is that, in English, both Latin and Greek expressions (like Anno Domini and kilometre) and English-based expressions are used fairly freely and sometimes they are mixed up.

Anno Domini dates from the days of Dionysius Exiguus in the 6th century, who more or less invented the basis of our current calendar. He got it about four years wrong, but it's understandable that Jesus was commemorated with a Latin phrase, Anno Domini, because it was the Roman emperor who asked for the job to be done.

The idea of referring to years *before* Jesus was born is much more recent. The first generally known reference to a scale of time before Jesus didn't surface until the 17th century, and didn't become common until the 18th century. And, here's the rub, whereas AD seemed to stick, in Latin, other languages made up their own versions of the time before Jesus: Germans refer to it as *VC* (*vor Christus*) and French call it *AvJC* (*avant Jesus Christ*).

And since there are other major religions which don't attribute the same significance to Jesus, outside Christian circles you'll come across another expression instead of BC — BCE, meaning Before Common Era. Incidentally, AD usually goes before a date and BC after.

 What is the connection between the word *adult*, which is completely acceptable, and *adultery*, which is regarded with some suspicion?

Adult and adultery have two slightly different paths of development: adult is from the Latin meaning a grown-up person, but adultery is believed to come from another Latin origin, *alter*, meaning to debase or render impure. When that word went into French as *avouter* it developed the meaning to stain or defile.

Avouter drifted into English as adultery and by the time Shakespeare used the word it carried the French sense of a blot, a stain, or something extra which is not pure, as adulterate still does — 'milk adulterated with water'.

Eventually adultery came to mean anything spurious or counterfeit, including sex between a married person and a partner other than the legal spouse. Now its use seems to be confined to that sense only.

 Are there differences between: *airport, aerodrome, airfield* **and** *airstrip*?

In some ways they're all the same, places at which aircraft land and take off, but in other ways they're slightly different.

Words not only change meaning over the years, they're also subject to fashion. One example of the latter is airport and aerodrome. In the days when ports were only for ships, aerodrome was most used. But a slight change in emphasis took place and in general the current usage is:

Airport: a take-off and landing area for *civil* and *commercial* aviation with surfaced runways and passenger facilities.

Aerodrome: a take-off and landing area, usually for *private* planes and in general smaller than an airport.

Airfield: a take-off and landing area that usually has some permanent buildings. Often used to describe centres of *military* air traffic.

Airstrip: a cleared area for take-off and landing which may be temporary and does not have considerable passenger facilities.

Air terminal: a location, usually in a city, where passengers assemble in order to start the process for taking off at an airport.

Q **Where do the words *alas and alack* come from?**

They're quite different. *Alas* is the older: it started to be used in English in the 13th century and was taken from the Old French *ha-las*, meaning Oh wretched! Two hundred years later, in the 15th century, we gained the word alack, which actually means what it says — ah-plus-lack, loss.

Sometime about 500 years ago someone decided to strengthen the image of one by adding the other. Alas and alack translates into modern English as Oh wretched, oh lost.

Q **What is the origin of the word *alimony*?**

Although we're familiar with the word alimony apparently it is not actually part of New Zealand law. In this country the correct term is 'spousal maintenance', although the Attorney General says they mean exactly the same thing.

Alimony is from Latin: *alere*, to nourish, then *alimonia*, sustenance. It has the same origin as alimentary, as in canal — the passage of food and sustenance. So in the United States, when someone is awarded alimony, they're actually being awarded sustenance, since they are no longer with the spouse who used to provide it.

Q **Why do we say *All my eye and Betty Martin* — 'I don't believe it, that's nonsense'?**

It used to be thought that this was a corruption of an Italian prayer *An mihi beate martine*, addressed to the patron saint of beggars, but there is no such prayer, so that explanation was abandoned.

The more probable background is that for years the expression 'my eye' meant much the same as now when we say 'my foot': that's rubbish, tell me another, you're pulling my leg . . .

There's also a theory that at one time there was a London actress called Betty Martin who was well known for her outspokenness and directness, and that somehow adding her name to the expression doubled it and made it stronger — my eye, and Betty Martin. But in some parts of England they say all my eye and Peggy Martin, so that confuses an already confused issue. So we know what it means, but we aren't sure where it comes from.

 What is the origin of the phrase *all over bar the shouting*?

The expression means that eventual success is certain. The only theory is that it arose as a result of boxing matches where it became quite clear, long before the finish, which participant was going to win. But the winner is not the winner until the referee makes a formal declaration and, when he does do that, there will be shouting and noise from the crowd.

So over time, if it was abundantly clear what the final decision was going to be, people came to say that it was all over, bar the shouting.

From boxing this expression has spread to almost any situation where there is some sort of a battle going on, from an America's Cup to a general election, and you feel confident enough to predict the result.

 What does *alleluia* mean?

Alleluia is a Hebrew word, or rather words, combined to form an instruction. The main portion of the word is part of the Hebrew verb 'to praise'. The part we hear is the second person plural imperative case of the verb — 'you shall praise' — plus a symbolic word for God at the end, a shortened form of Jehovah. So the word means 'Now everyone must praise Jehovah'. God, that is; Jesus was way off in future history when the word alleluia first came into use.

Q **Why does *Alzheimer's* disease have that name?**

It's named after the man who identified and researched the condition. He was Dr Alois Alzheimer, who was born in Germany and became professor of psychiatry and neurology at the Polish University of Breslau in 1917. Ten years before that happened he clarified that, in some people, apart from the general slowing down of old age, an actual disease can affect the efficiency of the brain cells. The particular condition has been named after him, as Alzheimer's disease, or Alzheimer's syndrome.

Q **Where is the apostrophe in *America's Cup*?**

The cup was originally called the Hundred Guineas Cup and was first raced for in 1851 when the winning schooner was called *America*. In time, by popular usage, it was referred to as the America's Cup, with an apostrophe designating that it belonged to the boat called *America*. And, according to the *Encyclopaedia Britannica*, that's how the name has stayed.

Q **Why is the Navy sometimes called *the Andrew*?**

Andrew Miller was a famous press gang operator in Plymouth during the French Revolution and the Napoleonic Wars (at the end of 18th and the beginning of the 19th centuries). He was so successful that his victims, finding themselves reluctantly in the Navy, said they had been 'snatched by *the* Andrew' or snatched into *the* Andrew.

As well as that, his full name, Andrew Miller, was occasionally used to describe a warship and Andrew was sometimes used to describe a manservant — an Andrew.

What are people born in *Argentina* correctly called?

This is partly the old problem about words from one language being pronounced differently when they're said in another language. In its own language the country is called Republica Argentina. When referred to in English, the 'a' is often dropped off, an 'e' put in its place, and 'the' put in front — the Argentine.

The *Encyclopaedia of Peoples of the World* explains that a man living there is called an Argentino and a woman is an Argentina (like Filipina and Filipino). In plural, the people call themselves Argentine. But the *Encyclopaedia Britannica* confidently calls them Argentinians.

So, two authorities differ. Neither seems to be wrong.

Why do some people say *at this point in time*?

The expression started quite legitimately. When astronauts are communicating they have to give precise and exact information about their location and they specify the various measurements by distinguishing the difference between a location in space or in time. So, saying at this point in time has a perfectly legitimate technical ancestry.

But the expression caught on among people who were naturally bombastic and round about the 1970s they developed the habit of saying 'at this point in time' or 'at this particular point in time' when they simply meant now.

In strict etymological terms this is called an orotundity, meaning bombastic and elaborate, from the Latin for with rounded mouth — people who like saying five or six words where one would do.

How did the term *au pair* originate?

The practice of having a young woman in the house to help look after the children and yet to be more or less equal with the family and not treated as an employee appears to have originated in Germany. The Germans called such a girl the house daughter.

The English language used a French term to describe exactly the same situation: in French, the term *au pair* means on an equal footing. The word *pair* in French is the origin of our English word peer, as in peer group or peer pressure — people who are equal.

The term has been around in English for a long time, but it was first recorded in a dictionary with this meaning in 1928. Nowadays, the term is often extended to au pair girl and sometimes used as a verb, to au pair.

 Why is the word *Australasia* deemed to be a combined reference to Australia and New Zealand?

When you look back at how this happened, it turns out to be a mistake. It comes from a French word *Australasie*, dated to 1794 which, apparently, did originally refer to Australia and Asia.

Over time the meaning was modified to mean Australia and all its neighbouring islands. When New Zealand established an identity of its own, the word had another slight refinement of meaning, namely the nations of Australia and New Zealand, plus both countries' outlying islands.

The term was used frequently throughout the 19th century, when the district of New Zealand was included within the diocese of Australasia; for a time the colony of New Zealand was actually administered from New South Wales. So it's understandable that Australians came to favour the word because it more or less eliminated New Zealand.

But conversely, up to about the 1940s, there was also a feeling that the word Australasia was used by New Zealanders to link themselves with a more powerful neighbour.

By 1960, in his introduction to *The Penguin Book of New Zealand Verse*, Allen Curnow indicated that the word had outlived its usefulness and was seldom if ever used in the press. Nowadays, in ordinary language, it seems that the word is hardly ever used in

Australia and not very often in New Zealand. Most New Zealanders don't seem comfortable with it and most Australians have simply never heard of the word.

 Does the 1988 *Australian Constitution* list New Zealand as one of its states?

The Australian Constitution, established in 1901, actually says: 'The Commonwealth means the Commonwealth of Australia. The States shall mean *such of* the colonies of New South Wales, New Zealand, Queensland, Tasmania, Victoria, Western Australia, South Australia, including the Northern Territory of Australia as for the time being are parts of the Commonwealth *and such colonies or territories as may be admitted into or established by the Commonwealth as States.*'

So what is actually being said, in paraphrase, is that New Zealand may be admitted — it if wants to. The constitution doesn't list it as *already being* a state and it never has. And, according to the Australian High Commission in New Zealand, that sentence remains exactly the same in the current constitution — so the gate is still open.

 Why do Americans say *automobile*?

Automobile is a combination of Greek *auto* meaning self, and Latin *mobile*, meaning to move. The word is used commonly in the United States but the car as we know it is actually a German invention, and the German language often used the word *Automobil* to describe cars, and still does, so Americans may have picked it up straight from Germany.

Q Is an *avocado* really a pear?

No, not at all. It is from the laurel family and is native to the Andean region of South America and this is where the name comes from.

When explorers first noticed the avocado trees, with their blackish hanging fruit, they asked the natives what they were called and the locals told them their name for the fruit, which was *ahuacatl*, and that's more or less what the rest of the world now calls them.

What the explorers didn't realise at the time was what *ahuacatl* actually means: it's the South American native word for testicles, which the locals thought the avocados resembled. So every time you ask for avocados in the vegetable section, you're actually asking for testicles. It's a clear case of getting away with saying something fairly indelicate as long as you say it in another language.

B

Q **Where does the expression *I bags that* come from?**

In late Middle English the word bag first became used as a verb: to put into a bag, to shoot game and put it into a bag. During the 19th century the verb grew another meaning: to reserve, to claim, especially on the grounds of being the first. It also developed a peculiar ending. Instead of *I bag this* — meaning I declare that this is going in my bag — the saying became *I bags this* or, in reverse for something you don't want, 'I bags not.'

Q **If *Mac* means son of, then what does *Bal* mean?**

Bal is the contemporary English spelling of an Old Gaelic word *bala*, which means place of, or settlement, as in Balmacewan — the place where the Macewans live.

There is a similar version in Irish Gaelic, e.g. the TV show *Ballykissangel*. Before you rush into asking whether Balmoral means place of the morals — no, not quite. *Moral* in Old Gaelic has the meaning of big, stately, the gentry, so the name Balmoral carries the connotation of place of the gentry.

Q **Where does the word *balderdash* come from?**

The word balderdash is a bit mysterious but it is associated with drink. The actual origin of the word itself is unknown, but in the 16th century the word was used to describe frothy liquid, and then it came to mean a mixture of liquids — leftovers, slops, often liquids that shouldn't be mixed and couldn't be drunk. So by the late 17th century people had extended the use of the word to mean not just messy liquid but anything useless, nonsensical, or trash.

Q If someone is *bandicooting*, what are they doing?

It's an Australian expression, referring to an animal called a bandicoot rat that causes mayhem in gardens by burrowing and eating tuberous vegetables such as potatoes, leaving the tops showing above the ground. The word bandicoot is a corruption of a Telugu word from India, meaning pig rat: the bandicoot makes a noise like a pig and then eats.

Since about 1920 the term bandicooting has been used in Australia to mean stealing, especially when it is not immediately obvious.

Q Why does a *bash* mean a party?

Bash is believed to come from a combination of bang and smash. Around 1930 the word began to be used to describe the loud and cheerful playing of dance music, and the noise of a party going with it. Eventually the notion of music all but disappeared from the meaning, and by the time it got to New Zealand in the 1940s, bash meant a party, celebration, a festivity, whether it has music or not.

Q Where does the word *bastard* come from?

There is an old word *bast* in English, meaning coarse plant fibre in a raw state before it is wound up into rope or string. People used to tie garden plants to stakes with bast, because it didn't cut into soft stems the way rope would.

Then there's also the old Latin word *bastum* meaning saddle. There's no established connection between the two, but there is a connection between the Latin and the English word bastard. In ancient times, there grew a French expression — *fils de bast*, child of a saddle — which referred to a child born of an unmarried mother, whose father had been a travelling herder, shepherd or muleteer, who probably used his saddle as a pillow, and then afterwards slung it back on his mule and rode away.

Two things happened to the French expression. The association between transient saddles and children with transient fathers gradually extended to be used about any child born out of wedlock, and the French was modified into the English version, bastard — a child born from a saddle rather than a marriage bed.

 Why is an officer's soldier-servant called a *batman*?

It has nothing to do with bats. The word comes from an old French word, which itself comes from the Latin *bastum*, which means packsaddle.

In early times, the batman was the soldier in charge of the packhorse carrying the officer's luggage. Eventually packhorses weren't used so much in the military and it is believed that, during the First World War, non-regular officers used the term quite erroneously to describe an officer's servant and the usage stuck.

 How did the expression *wait with bated breath* originate?

It's all in the spelling. Bated breath has nothing to do with fish bait and it mustn't be spelt that way. It's short for the word *abated*, which means made less, smaller in amount.

You hear it nowadays mainly in the contexts of weather or law: The storm abated, or that a court order has abated something, meaning that it's been removed, suppressed, annulled. But you don't hear the word much anywhere else, except in bated breath, which has dropped the first *a*, but is the same word. The breath is being held tight and not allowed to expand.

Q What is meant by *bearded like the pard*?

The origin is Shakespeare, from the famous Seven Ages of Man speech in *As You Like It*: 'Then a soldier, bearded like the pard, / Jealous in honour, sudden and quick in quarrel'.

Pard means a panther or leopard, but 'bearded like' isn't quite so straightforward. In earlier times beard didn't always mean the bit under the chin — it sometimes meant hair on the face generally. In Burke's *History of England*, 1757, he writes, 'Britons shaved the beard on the chin, but that on the upper lip was suffered to remain'. So when Shakespeare said 'bearded like the pard' he probably meant great bristling moustaches, like the whiskers on a leopard.

There is also another possibility. Another meaning of to beard survives into modern English as to face fearlessly, to beard someone in their den. So because Shakespeare was describing a soldier when he wrote that line, he might have meant as fierce as a leopard when it is confronted.

Either way, whether the man looks like a leopard, or is as formidable as an angered leopard, the image is one of bravery and courage.

Q Where did the expression *beer and skittles* originate?

Skittles is an ancient game, the ancestor of today's indoor or ninepin bowling. Traditionally it was accompanied by light-hearted activity — and drinking, usually of port. Charles Dickens mentions it in *Pickwick Papers*, which was serialised over 1836 to 1837.

But the alcohol seemed to go down-market in the next few years, and the expression in print had changed to beer and skittles by the time George Du Maurier wrote the novel *Trilby* in 1894. In that book you'll find the expression as we know it today — 'Life isn't all beer and skittles' — so port had become beer, and has remained so.

Where did the phrase *bee's knees* originate?

This nonsense phrase has no particular origin; it comes into the same category as cat's pyjamas. Bee's knees means 'the acme of perfection' and, according to Eric Partridge, has been in use since about 1930.

 Is the name *berley*, for the mixture of pollard and oil put out to attract fish, confined to New Zealand and Australia?

Both berley and burley seem to exist and the word is known to have been used in Australia since 1874.

The origin is not quite so straightforward. It seems possible that early Australians used the word to mean nonsense or rubbish, and it may be related to another Australasian expression 'to give it a burl', which itself is obscure but might be derived from give it a whirl. The truth is, however, that berley, meaning fish-bait, has to be described as origin unknown.

Well-known New Zealand fishing identity Bill Hohepa describes the word as a 'fisho original' that only became common in New Zealand in the 1980s. (Bill Hohepa doesn't use berley; he buys a tin of dog food, punches two holes in it and dangles it on a string in the water. It works well.)

 Why is New York often referred to as *the Big Apple*?

The expression is thought to have originated among Black American jazz musicians who, when they got an engagement in a big city, referred to it in various versions of the phrase 'bite of the apple', meaning a chance at success. (This was similar to a 'bite of the cherry'.)

New York, of course, was the biggest city, so it became the Big Apple. An advertising man latched onto the jazz phrase and began to use it in advertising about New York.

Q **What is the origin of the expression** *big girl's blouse?*

This is usually said to a man, and tells him that he's weak, indecisive, shy — and here's the operative word — and soft. The expression is not uncommon in New Zealand and you'll also hear it occasionally on *Coronation Street*, because that's the area it comes from — North England.

The verb to blouse something has been in use for some time in certain circumstances, and simply means to fill with air. Why? Because, traditionally, a woman's blouse is made of soft fabric, and although it is filled with a woman, there is also a certain amount of air in there as well. And if the blouse is too big for the girl wearing it then of course there is more air in it than girl.

In the world of machismo — which is the Mexican word for strong maleness — men are not supposed to be soft creatures. The Sensitive New Age Guy may be gentle and considerate and caring, but there is still a very strong professional All Black-type image that a real man is tough and hard. That image has not changed at all — if anything, it has intensified.

So to call a man a blouse, or a girl's blouse, implies that he is malleable, gentle, floppy, and that can be amplified by adding big. (Note that it's the blouse, not the girl, who is big, and therefore the blouse is even floppier.)

Q **What is the origin of** *bigot?*

Some people will tell you that it's a contraction of 'By God', meaning that what this person is stating is the only possible view to have. But the history of the word doesn't support that because it's actually French in origin . . . and not saying By God, because it wouldn't sound like that in French.

It's a racist word, like bugger. (This was originally a corruption of Bulgarian, used as a pejorative term across Europe to describe certain unapproved religious sects. The term was extended to other outsiders, usually sexual, and eventually became an expletive of shock, distaste and then just surprise.)

Nobody is sure exactly how bigot arose, but it was a contemptuous word the ancient French used with reference to the Normans because they had different ways of doing things. And from that it drifted into English to describe someone who stubbornly believes that their own views are the only ones possible, and that everyone else is wrong.

 Is it true that the word *bimbo* is an example of an expression that has reversed its meaning?

It has reversed because bimbo means boy. It's an Italian word, short for *bambino*. (In Italian, when a word ends in an o it's masculine.) There even used to be a song about it — 'Bimbo bimbo where y' going to goi-o . . . going down the street, to meet a little girlio.' In Italian, a little girl is called a *bambina*, or *bimba*.

Why on earth the English language has adopted the word bimbo from Italian, but reversed its gender, nobody knows. But just be careful if you're in Italy — don't refer to a pretty girl as a bimbo because you're actually implying she's a bloke dressed up as a girl.

 Birds are often quite smart, so why does *bird brain* usually mean someone is stupid?

The expression is believed to derive from the assumption that, because birds' heads in general seem very small in proportion to their bodies, their brains must be tiny. It isn't necessarily true, but bird brain also has a pleasing alliteration, so because of those two factors it's often used to mean someone dizzy or with a short attention span.

 Why do New Zealand racehorses appear in the *birdcage* before a race, when overseas the same thing is described as the parade ring?

Well, the short answer is, nobody knows. And when I say nobody, I'm including racing writer John Costello, whose authoritative book *Tapestry of Turf* tells you everything you always wanted to know about New Zealand racing — except that bit.

I'm also including Pat Finnegan, who is historian to the Racing Museum and has read, written or researched every item concerning the history of horseracing in New Zealand. His answer to the question is 'Nobody knows. There are about 100 explanations to this question, none of them proven. Everyone has a different version but they can't be taken seriously as a researched fact.' Pictures of the Riccarton course in the 1870s clearly show what we nowadays call a birdcage, but there is no explanation for the use of the word. It has nothing to do with the word birdcage used to describe railway carriages with open sides, because they came much later; there were racecourses in New Zealand long before there were trains.

You won't hear it at Ascot, Goodwood, Epsom, Santa Monica or any other famous international racecourse; the term is unknown anywhere but New Zealand.

 Does the London street called *Birdcage Walk* have anything to do with horses parading, or with birds?

Definitely birds. Unlike many strange names in England, this one means exactly what it says. The street has been called that for over 300 years, and it's believed to have come about because Charles II established aviaries of exotic birds there. Most of the creatures died in London's cold weather, but the name remains.

Q **Why is *bitch* a derogatory term for women?**

The word bitch comes originally from Scandinavia and has been in English for several centuries. For the last 500 years it has also been used as a derogatory word for malicious or treacherous women, but there's no clear answer as to why.

Bitch means female dog, but it's also used as the female for wolf and fox. It's generally conceded that dogs of either gender are fairly companionable, but wolves and foxes often aren't. So it is remotely possible that years ago when people called someone malicious a bitch, they may have had wolves and foxes in mind, just as much as dogs.

Interestingly enough, for a very long time bitch was a derogatory term for men as well as women, through to the 19th century and up until comparatively recently. Robert Louis Stevenson used the word to describe a man in one of his books, as did James Joyce.

In general, however, the word seems to have settled on women — Shakespeare used it that way — and nobody really knows how it started.

 A Scottish grandmother used sometimes to say she was *black affronted*. Why?

In Scotland one of the many subtle shades of meaning for the word black is extreme as in, for instance, black shame or black disgrace. This grandmother used to use the word when she was severely embarrassed: 'I was black affronted' meant 'I was very embarrassed'.

 They had a *black dog on their back*. Where does that idea come from?

It's a very old idea indeed: it's referred to in the writings of the Latin poet Horace over 2000 years ago and it has cropped up in various versions ever since.

The basic idea was that the devil was able to assume the shape of a black dog. This was compounded in the ancient Roman belief that it was very bad luck to see a black dog with her puppies. And when someone has a gloomy disposition, it can be said that a black dog has walked over him.

So having a black dog on your back means that you're feeling full of gloom and woe and the devil, who is causing it, cannot be shaken off.

 The black ox hath trod on her foot and the crow hath set its footprints about her eyes. Where does this quote come from?

It was first published as a proverb in 1546, and then reappeared in 1584 in John Lyly's *Sapho and Phao*. In that version it says: 'Nor crow's foot is on her eye, and the black ox hath trod on her foot'.

 Where does the expression _this side of the black stump_ come from?

It's an Australian expression dating from the mid-1930s. There is only one vague explanation, namely that in the Australian bush and outback, people customarily gave directions by naming natural features such as a rock, a river, an outstanding tree — or a stump. So 'this side of the black stump' means not very far away and 'beyond the black stump' means a long way away, but the general connotation for both is of fairly remote territory.

 What is the origin of _Blighty_, meaning England?

Blighty comes from an Urdu word *b'layti*, meaning a foreign place. Military men who'd served in the Middle East picked up the word and during the First World War it came to mean England. A blighty or a blighty one was a wound that would ensure a soldier got sent home to England.

When a director is described as *blocking* a scene (deciding what actors must do and where they are to move to) wouldn't it be more logical to say he or she is setting the scene?

In fact, both terms are used in the theatre, occasionally interchangeably, but block is the word usually used when a director is just starting to plan out exactly where everyone will stand and where they will move to.

There are over 40 different meanings for the word block and this one appears to have evolved from the practice many directors have of starting from a drawing of the stage, onto which they pencil the divisions of the acting areas or blocks. When the actors eventually assemble, the director can then start moving them around to make interesting groupings, or to ensure that a certain character is prominent at an important moment, and to keep the stage picture changing so that characters aren't standing in the same places for too long. They're being moved from block to block. Once the movements and groupings are finalised the word blocking usually ceases to be used and the meetings then become rehearsals.

The expression to set the scene can sometimes mean something similar, as in to set the table or to set the fire, where you arrange certain things in a way that will use them effectively. But in theatre that expression usually has a slightly different connotation: you arrange certain incidents and props and lighting in order to highlight something that's coming up. It's almost as if you should say setting up a scene, because it's leading to something else.

 Where do we get the word *blue*, as in making a mistake?

The expression is believed to be Australian but there is no certainty as to its exact origin. Eric Partridge points out that there are many meanings for the word *blue*. In the 18th century the meaning was to *blush*, by the mid-19th century blue could mean to spend wastefully and by 1880 to miscalculate. All of those more or less add up to making a blue. And in Australia a blue is a fight.

Also relevant is the fact that court summonses were printed on blue paper. Blue might also be an abbreviated form of bloomer, meaning a mistake, which has been in use since at least 1954.

 Why are studious women called *bluestockings*?

The term itself dates back to the 15th century, when intellectuals used to meet in Venice and deliberately wore blue-coloured stockings. The idea later surfaced in Paris in the 1500s and women were prominent within that group. By the 18th century a similar set-up had started in England, where a women-only group met for discussion — which was thought a little unusual. But those groups continued into the 19th century, and at times the women would invite eminent men such as Horace Walpole and Charles Dickens to special meetings. One man declined because he didn't think he was appropriately dressed and was told to just come as he was — so he did, wearing ordinary blue-grey daytime stockings. So for various reasons bluestockings has been associated with intellectual thinkers for 500 years.

The term has a negativity about it which isn't easily explained except by the fact that for many years males of the species were very reluctant to concede that females might be clever. So the term bluestockings was used fairly dismissively about women with brains, many of whom actually did wear blue stockings, with the connotation that they were probably plain and dull. This wasn't, and still isn't, always true.

 Why is a funny flat straw hat called *a boater*?

A boater is a hat for wearing while on a boat!

Q **Why do people say *Bob's your uncle* when they wish to point out that something is easily achieved or all will be well?**

The expression is British and has been in use since the 1880s. There's only one theory about the possible origin of the phrase. In 1886, the Prime Minister of Britain, Robert Cecil, appointed his nephew Arthur Balfour first as President of the Local Government Board and then as Secretary for Scotland with a seat in the Cabinet. The following year he was given the highly prestigious post of Chief Secretary of Ireland.

Robert Cecil was Arthur Balfour's Uncle Bob, so researcher Nigel Rees thinks the phrase may have grown from the gossip that when you had an influential Uncle Bob, things would go well with you.

Q **Why is the word *Bohemia* also used to describe a lifestyle?**

Bohemia was a country, and immigrants came from there to New Zealand. But hundreds of years before that, it was believed that gypsy people were based there and the word Bohemia began to take on the connotation of people living casually and unconventionally.

Many art students in Paris did live like that, even when they weren't from Bohemia, and the word *bohemian*, meaning unconventional and arty, gradually entered the international consciousness. In 1847–48 Thackeray used the word in *Vanity Fair* to describe Becky Sharp's parents — 'wild, roving and Bohemian'.

But something else happened about the same time — writer Henri Murger wrote his novel *Scenes of a Bohemian Life* about French art students living in an unconventional way. That book was the basis of an opera, Puccini's *La Bohème*, which became very famous indeed, and ever since the word bohemian has meant an arty kind of life. In the meantime the country that was Bohemia had become part of Czechoslovakia.

The nickname *Bohunk* is unpleasant, but what does it actually mean?

It's an old-fashioned politically incorrect term meaning someone from Eastern Europe: it blends *Bo*(hemian) with *Hunk*(arian). There's an old American song, 'Bohunkus', about a farmer with a clumsy son. The term isn't heard much nowadays.

 What is the origin of the word *boncer*?

This comes from an old British dialect word *boncer* or *bouncer*, meaning a big marble (shortened in British slang to bonce, meaning the head). Because the marble was big, and therefore rather splendid in comparison with other marbles, the word bouncer or boncer came to be used to mean things that were splendid or superior.

Then along came the word bonanza, from a different source: the Latin *bonus*, meaning good. *Bonanza* grew in use in America, originally applied to a mine, rich in ore, that made its owner wealthy. And a kind of melding took place so that boncer (with a c) gradually became bonzer, meaning great, outstanding, sudden and unexpected riches.

So you have bouncer, boncer, bonsa, bonza and bonzer, all of which are variations on the same idea and all mean the same thing: splendid.

Katherine Mansfield used the word — she wrote about a fine house with a boncer garden, and you'll find it with two spellings: one edition has boncer and another has bonzer.

 Where does the slang phrase *up the booai* or *boohai* come from?

In the 19th century a number of immigrants came to New Zealand from Bohemia and many of them went to live in a small settlement north of Auckland called Puhoi.

Because their English was a bit tentative and Maori words were unfamiliar, they had difficulty with the name of Puhoi, and also because, as a group, they were considered colourful and exotic, the mispronunciation *booai* came to mean a remote and mystical place that not many ordinary people ever saw.

There are many variants such as 'up the booai shooting pukekos' or even 'up the boohai for the rhubarb season', but all derive from Puhoi.

 Whatever is *Bookbinder soup*?

The name conjures up an image of thick white paste, possibly made from a lot of potatoes or, even worse, a sticky brown mixture made from boiled horses' hooves — like the glue bookbinders use.

But no, it's an American recipe, named after a family called Bookbinder, who ran some well-known restaurants. They made a characteristic soup that is in fact red, because it's based on a tomato broth, in which pieces of red snapper are cooked. It could be classified as a chowder and sometimes seems to include clams.

A bowl of Bookbinder soup is very rich, and it isn't cheap: it would cost the equivalent of $NZ15. It is usually served as part of a seafood meal, and would be followed by smoked salmon or crab cakes.

 Why do we say 'He's very clever, and handsome *to boot*'?

We use it only when we're saying two things about a situation. To boot is an Old English expression meaning in addition to or as well, from an ancient word boot, meaning to compensate or counter-balance two pieces of information that aren't connected with each other.

Q Can you provide some background to the expression *a Boston marriage?*

The phrase is heard only occasionally, usually in the United States. It means that two women are living together, independently of any financial support from a man. This can sometimes be a lesbian relationship but not necessarily. It is not uncommon for single women from the academic professions to share housing and, being university or school teachers, or writers or artists, they can of course make a living without there being any husband in the equation.

If they continue to live together after retirement, the arrangement is sometimes referred to as a Boston marriage, whether they are sexual partners or not. A Boston marriage can simply be an arrangement of convenience and companionship between women who have like interests and don't get on each others nerves.

The expression arose in the United States after the publication of Henry James's novel *The Bostonians* in 1886. This book featured two strong-minded women of lively intellect who shared each other's lives — at least to a certain extent.

Such arrangements have been carried out for centuries, but the expression Boston marriage, and the other expression 'romantic friendship', date from the decades when the word lesbian was never mentioned and Queen Victoria said it didn't exist. The phrase found renewed usage recently after David Mamet wrote a new play called *A Boston Marriage*, which concerned two outspoken women.

Q Why does *'He's bought it'* mean he's died?

Some people think the expression is an abbreviated form of 'He's bought the farm', but the stories vary. 'Bought the farm' is an American expression relating to the use of the word farm (as opposed to ranch) meaning dirt farm for growing crops and thus endless digging, like graves.

Another version thinks bought the farm relates to Second World War servicemen, particularly men from the Navy, who, when they retired, got as far away from the sea as possible. When anyone asked where they were, the reply was 'they've bought a farm' meaning they'd left the sea and gone a long way away. And eventually this also came to mean they'd died.

Either of those is possible, but the only honest answer is that nobody is totally sure.

Q Where does the word *bounder* originate?

Like cad, bounder means someone capable of ungentlemanly behaviour, but its ancestry is a bit different. Originally it simply meant an animal that leapt about a lot.

Social conventions have always been very strongly held in British life, and anyone who broke The Rules was bound to get themselves talked about. People who did break the rules, usually men, were seen as having bounded over the conventions or bounded away from normal behaviour. During the 19th century this term took hold but, curiously, it was more or less confined to men in the higher reaches of society. It was usually said only about well-dressed men who normally kept elegant company, but tended to be offensive, vulgar and irrepressible, particularly about women.

Q What is the origin of *box of birds*?

One etymologist describes this as a 'pleasing alliteration', rather like the similar phrase fighting fit (which originally meant what it said). The phrase has been in use since about 1939 and is thought to have originated with the New Zealand troops in the Second World War.

Q Why do we often describe something as *brand spanking new*?

Here two different expressions have merged. Brand in this case means the hot logo from the forge which is used to burn a sign into cattle and other articles. When a thing has just been branded, the mark is clearly visible, not overgrown or weathered, so it is brand new. Shakespeare used a version of the expression when he called something 'fire new'.

Spanking is a dialect word from the 17th century which meant fit and lively, exceptionally showy and striking; it was often used to describe a dashing horse who moved briskly.

The two expressions merged somehow, and the impact was doubled.

 Q Did *brass monkeys* have their balls frozen off or on?

The rack of brass or bronze on which a ship's cannon balls sat was known as a brass monkey. Some people steeped in marine tradition feel strongly that, in low temperatures, the balls became frozen but stayed where they were — so saying the balls froze off is indeed a semantic reversal.

But others are equally convinced that because iron balls freeze at a different temperature from their brass or bronze housing, then the balls, when frozen, no longer fitted into their indentations, and rolled off all over the deck. Thus, freezing weather did cause the balls to fall off the brass monkey.

Yet a third explanation is that ice surrounding the balls pushed them a little bit apart and slightly out of kilter with their indentations. When warmer winds meant that the ice melted, and no longer held them, the balls would respond by falling about.

So marine scholars agree only that cold weather can freeze the balls on or off a brass monkey, and semantic reversal has nothing to do with it.

How did *parted brass rags*, meaning an unamicable separation, come about?

The expression is thought to have originated among sailors, who kept a particular pile of old rags just for cleaning brass — because such cloths became dirty and smelly and weren't used to clean down anything else. Thus, if the phrase brass rags means that something is unpleasant and disagreeable, parted brass rags means a separation that is acrimonious.

 Why do theatre people say *break a leg* to each other before a show?

This way of wishing good luck in the theatre is an old custom and has nothing to do with the famous actress Sarah Bernhardt, who actually did have a wooden leg.

There are two aspects to the probable origin of this theatre expression. First, for many centuries people have believed that you might be able to avert an unexpected unpleasant event if you pretended to foresee it as a facetious wish. It still happens in ordinary life when you hear some people say, 'I don't want it to rain today — so I'll take an umbrella with me.' The premise is that if you don't take an umbrella it *will* rain, and if you do take an umbrella, it won't.

In line with that old superstition, there was an old Yiddish expression originating in German — 'Hals and Beinbruch' — which, although it means 'Neck and leg both broken', was actually said to people to wish them luck.

There's no exact reference that the theatre tradition did uplift the old Yiddish or German phrase but it is widely believed that one is a condensed version of the other. If you say 'break a leg' to someone who's about to go out on the stage and give a performance, what you're really saying is, 'I hope things go well for you and you don't have any accidents that could jeopardise the performance.'

Q *Buckley's chance* means no chance at all.
Who was Buckley?

Life of Reilly, Murphy's Law, Davy Jones's locker, happy as Larry
— sometimes these people are real, but sometimes they become
lost or are mythical.

There are several explanations about Buckley's chance. The
most widely believed one is that there was an outlaw called Buckley
in Australia over a century ago, and such was the determination
and force of the law used to catch him that people said he had no
chance of escape. This grew into an expression since about 1875,
and Buckley's chance is now commonly used to mean a situation
or person without any hope.

 Q What are *bugger grips*?

In earlier decades men used to grow their whiskers into
what are sometimes called sideboards, sideburns or mutton chops.
But there was a vague feeling that this affectation belonged to the
upper classes rather than the lower, and this was the case at sea,
where officers and gentlemen tended to grow whiskers on the
sides of the face and the cheeks. These were referred to as bugger
grips by the sailors of the lower decks. So, it's naval slang.

 Q Why are both the human posterior and an
American tramp called *a bum*?

The human posterior has been called a bum for 600 years and the
reason why that word crept into use simply isn't clear. It might,
however, be a sort of visual version of onomatopoeia, in that the
shape of the word itself seems very appropriate — a short, plump,
round word. There is also a strong possibility that bum is an
abbreviated form of bottom.

The American tramp meaning is a lot clearer, because it's
believed to be derived from the German word *bummler*, meaning

useless or idle. So in English, a bum was originally a dawdler or loafer, and it's travelled a bit from there, at least in American English, to mean a person who is so idle they don't have a job, and from there to meaning someone who roams around without the stability of a home or employment.

There's also a breath of influence from Britain, where bum is sometimes used to describe a person who is idle and sits on their bum a lot.

Q **What about *bum steer*, *bum rap* and *bum's rush*?**

They all appear to have come into the language from somewhere in North America where the old word bum originally had a flavour of disapproval — a dawdler, a useless person. So the word bum had a connotation of being bad — hence bad advice or bad treatment could be implied by putting the word bum at the beginning of an expression. We even say something is bum when it won't work properly.

Q **Where does the expression *going butcher's hook* come from?**

This was originally Cockney rhyming slang — butcher's hook rhymes with look, so to take a butcher's hook means to take a look — and in the usual way with rhyming slang the second word is often dropped off, so it becomes take a butcher's.

Australia and New Zealand have developed a secondary rhyming slang where butcher's hook rhymes with crook — in the sense of angry, disagreeable. So in Australia and New Zealand, going butcher's hook, or just going butcher's, means going crook.

***Butt* or *buck* naked — which is correct?**

Butt naked is possibly derived from buttock naked. Buck naked may be related to the slang for dollar and probably dates from a time when deer skins were classified as bucks and does, and bucks were worth more.

Funk & Wagnall says 'buck' is American slang for skin. Ask any American and they'll say buck naked is the usual expression.

There is also buff naked, which is probably derived from the buff-coloured shorts worn by some of the armed forces in hot weather — frequently with nothing else. Although they weren't actually naked, the term was extended to describe them when they actually were. The expression survives mainly as in the buff.

Q **Why do men's clothes always have their *buttons* on the right and women's on the left?**

There are several different versions of the reason for this, but this is the usually accepted one.

Buttons originated in the 13th century. In the 15th century men, particularly in battle, dressed themselves, so their buttons were on the right because most men were right-handed.

Women who could afford to, had servants. (And because, in those times, buttons were very decorative and expensive, most women who had buttons at all also had maids.) So customarily, buttons on women's clothes were the mirror image of men's so that a right-handed maid could face the clothes and button them easily.

Tailors caught on to this and made it normal practice to put men's buttons on their right, and women's on their left.

Q **Where on earth did the expression** *by and large* **originate?**

It didn't originate on earth at all. By and large has a nautical origin; it dates from at least 1670. To sail by and large is to sail close to the wind and slightly off it, thus making it easier for the helmsman to steer and less likely for the vessel to be taken aback. In other words, it means to keep a ship on course so that it is sailing a good speed even though the direction of the wind is changing. The expression now means 'generally speaking' which, I suppose, is very roughly equivalent! By and large, meaning generally speaking, has been used by landlubbers since the 19th century.

C

Q Left-handed is often referred to as *cack-handed*.
Why?

For some time cack has been a fairly common vernacular term for excrement. Excrement is usually messy. People who are clumsy often find it difficult to be tidy, so the expression cack-handed really arose to describe anyone who had a clumsy, untidy way of doing things. It was not very complimentary — and not very formal — but definitely part of the language.

I once overheard two women sharing dishwashing duties and one told the other that she was doing it cack-handed — because she washed from the bottom of the pile to the top. Her technique was different from her helper's, and seemed messy so she was called cack-handed. But it didn't mean that she was left-handed and was intended as banter, not an insult.

Once source refers to the fact that the expression came into wide use among the armed forces. Servicemen in some Asian areas discovered that toilet paper was unknown there and consequently there was a customary division of duties between the left and the right hand: the right hand was always used for handling food, and the left hand was designated to do what toilet paper does in other cultures.

I'm suggesting that the British servicemen who came across that interesting fact were already familiar with the term cack-handed, meaning clumsy, and some bright spark extended it: the left hand being the cack hand, then left-handed people were cack-handers, whether they were Asians or not.

Currently, I think, the old meaning still prevails: a person wrestling with a computer keyboard and getting it all wrong can be described as cack-handed, because they're clumsy. Left-handed people are not necessarily clumsy at all but, in a moment of jokey put-down, can sometimes be referred to as cack-handers, because of the Other Reason.

Q **What is the origin of the word *cad*?**

Cad is an abbreviation of caddie or caddy, which itself derived from the French word *cadet*. It's believed that this word was introduced to Britain by Mary Queen of Scots — she came from France, and was a very keen golfer. But one way or another, the word cadet slowly changed to caddie, which had several meanings: a caddie was not only someone who carried the clubs during a golf game but also an errand boy and someone who hitched rides on carriages without paying the full fare.

Gradually the word divided into two — caddie remained fixed to golfing duties and was quite respectable, but the shorter version, cad, carried with it the connotation of people jumping onto the backs of carriages and hitching a ride, so it was applied to bad boys and vulgar men, capable of ungentlemanly behaviour. Bounder is a similar term.

Q **Why is the container for tea called a *caddy*?**

Caddy comes from the Malayan word *kati* which is a unit of weight, just over half a kilogram — roughly a pound — so a pound of tea was a *kati* and somehow that became the name of the box or tin in which it was kept.

Q **Why do we say 'You can't have your *cake* and eat it too?**

The expression is commonly put back to front from its original. In this context, the word have means keep — to simultaneously eat your cake but also keep it — which isn't normally possible.

The saying has been in use since the 16th century. It appears in print in 1546 in John Heywood's *Proverbs* in its original version — 'Both eat your cake and have your cake'. The expression was used of people who, for example, behaved with religious purity one day a week, and then were ruthless landlords and business sharks on the other days. They were serving God and Mammon at the same time — they had two opposing advantageous things going on at once. The phrase was almost one of envy.

Over time, two things happened: first, the saying somehow became reversed and second, it changed into the negative. So instead of saying 'Eat your cake and have it', which was a statement of envy, people began to say 'You can't have your cake and eat it', which is a statement of admonishment, and the current version.

 What does *Calathumpian* mean?

The word's ancestry is not clear but it appears to derive from a similar word beginning with G — Gallithumpians — which was apparently the name of a social reform movement ages ago. The G seems to have migrated into a C.

Calathumpian is used in slightly different ways by different people but the pattern is the same: it's always a put-down about someone else's religion. Some people say it about Calvinists, others use it about atheists, or Jews or Catholics.

It's a bit like the word pagan, which is often used to describe any religion other than your own. And that's more or less what Calathumpian means — any religion that you, the speaker, do not hold in respect. It is perceived as a rather offensive word.

Why does the disease *cancer* have a name connected with a crab?

The disease we call cancer was known well over 2000 years ago, and it was named by Hippocrates, often called the father of medicine. He used the ancient Greek word for crab — *karkinos*

— but not because of how the disease felt to the sufferer.

The cancers Hippocrates was able to identify were malignant tumours that had horrible veins stretching out from them so he called them *karkinos* because they *looked* like a crab. The Greek word was modified by the Latin language into the word *cancer*, and has remained that way ever since.

There is an echo of the Greek *karkinos* in the other word, canker, which is still used but seems to be applied more to animals and plants than to humans.

There is also the sign of the zodiac known as cancer, which doesn't actually look much like a crab. It's called that because of an ancient legend that Hercules was bitten by a crab while he was fighting the beast Hydra, and Hercules crushed the crab. So one of Hercules' enemies, Hera, rewarded the creature for having tackled Hercules, by giving the crab a place in the heavens — and the constellation of stars with that name travels backwards and sideways, like a crab.

In recent times there has been some resistance to the name cancer being used as a zodiac sign and there is a move in the United States to replace it with the name Moon Child.

 What is *canola oil*?

It is oil from a crop called rape. The change of name resulted from the Canadian producers of cooking oil deciding to rename the product because rape oil had an unattractive connotation. So *can* (for Canada) combined with *ola* (oil) made a new word and that was that.

The same thing happened with tamarillo, which used to be tree tomato. It is made-up word starting with tomato — changed to *tama* to give a Maori feel to the word — and adding *illo* to suggest that it is small. The new name has been universally accepted.

Kiwi fruit, too was renamed deliberately. The fruit's real name in Chinese is actually monkey peach and we used to call it Chinese gooseberry, but we all now call it kiwi fruit.

Is *car* short for *cart*?

There are four words about transport vehicles that sound similar: chariot, cart, car and carriage.

Chariot, cart and car are closely related; they've come into English through Old French in the two forms *carre* and *carete*, which ultimately originate from the Latin *carrum*, which was a kind of wagon. It's not quite right to say that car is short for cart; they *are* related but one is not intended to be a short version of the other.

Carriage also comes from Old French but from the word *carier*, to carry, so its ancestry is marginally different.

 Chemists once had beautiful big glass jars, usually coloured, called *carboys*. How did the name arise?

The jars had nothing to do with cars or with boys. The word originated in Persia (now Iran): *karaba* simply meant a big jar, especially one that could hold acid and corrosive liquids — and glass will resist most of those. The Persian word was adopted into the English language about 200 years ago and is still there, though very few chemists seem to have carboys now.

 What does the word *carol* actually mean?

Carol comes from an Old French word that actually meant singing and *dancing* while standing in a circle, so early Christmas carols were much more lively and rambunctious than we think of them now.

Nowadays, the word carol has diverged into three separate divisions — (1) genuine old Christmas carols such as 'God Rest ye Merry, Gentlemen' and 'Oh, Come all ye Faithful', (2) Christmas hymns, which are rather less lively, and (3) songs that are somehow about Christmas but don't actually mention Jesus, such as 'Santa Claus is Coming to Town' or 'Rudolph the

Red-Nosed Reindeer'. These are not carols, but Christmas songs.

Q **What is the origin of the expression** *to let the cat out of the bag?*

For years this expression has meant to reveal a secret, or put about damaging information that was supposed to be confidential. There are two schools of thought about its origin. Some scholars say it is directly related to the pig in the poke — if the buyer demanded that the vendor actually show him the squealing animal within the poke, then he'd see a cat; a secret would be revealed, and the cat would be out of the bag.

But there is also a parallel explanation arising from the old-time shipboard practice of punishing sailors with an evil whip known as a cat-o'-nine-tails. When a sailor was summoned for some misdemeanour, and he saw that the cat had been removed from the pouch it was kept in and was lying ready for use, then the cat was out of the bag and he knew that something unpleasant was about to happen.

Take your pick.

Q **Where does the word** *census* **come from?**

It doesn't mean hundreds. The practice of taking a census, which is the numbers of population and also their ages, sex, financial condition etc., dates back to ancient Rome, and the name comes from the Roman word *censere*, meaning to assess. A census is not only a counting, it is an assessment.

Q **Is** *chairman* **really a sexist word?**

The 'man' in chairman is from the Latin *manus* which specifically means hand but has the strong connotation of power. We hear the basic Latin word for hand in several surviving languages: Italian and Spanish *mano*, French *main*.

In English 'manus' survives in words like manual. But the connotation of hand meaning power also survives in such words as manager (which has nothing to do with being a man, but means the power of administering) and emancipate (which means to give power). We hear the connotation of the hand having power in such expressions as 'The hand of God' or 'The hand of the Prime Minister could be seen in . . .'.

By coincidence, the English word man, meaning male, looks the same as the Latin derivation man, meaning hand or power of the hand. So 'chairman' refers to the power of the person holding a superior office in an organisation and it doesn't really mean the person is male. The word has been in use since 1654.

There is no real need for words like chairwoman or chairperson; chairman would do. But it must be acknowledged there has been confusion for some time, and the word chairwoman has also been used for many years. The judge at the David Bain trial had a neat solution: he addressed the jury spokesperson as Madame Foreman, which sounded absolutely right.

Q **What is the difference between *chutney* and *relish*?**

Not much, just words. Relish was originally a French word, used by the English since 1530 to describe special enjoyment, usually something that was available occasionally as a treat and might not last long — even as nowadays you can relish swimming in summer. By the late 1600s, relish had also come to mean something special and tasty added to the dinner table — again, a little treat.

Later, when the British started travelling to India a lot, they brought back spicy mixtures in jars, known by the Hindi word *chutni*. This was always chopped-up sweet fruit treated with acids, sour herbs and hot flavourings. Mango chutney was the big one, and still is. Gradually, the new-fangled *chutni* became the attractive thing added to the dinner table, rather than the relish. And the two words became more or less interchangeable.

There are some people who insist that there is a difference, that real chutneys are made with a fruit as the main ingredient, whereas relishes are made with vegetables, but food experts concede that there really isn't a difference.

Q **Why are farmers often called *cockies* or *cow cockies*?**

Early European dwellers in Australia were intrigued that, no matter how remote or unfriendly a terrain was, there were always cockatoos there. And because city people were often dismayed at the arid conditions in which farmers earned their livelihood, they began referring to farmers as cockatoos, which was contracted to cockies.

Q **Where does the word *codswallop* come from?**

There's no definite scholastic proof about the origin of the word codswallop, but the generally accepted version goes like this.

Besides the usual meanings of wallop, in 19th-century Britain the word was also used as a slang term meaning beer. Round about 1875 a man called Hiram Codd took out a patent for a kind of bottle that could hold bubbles inside because it contained a marble that 'stoppered' it. The bottles were used for selling mineral water, which was fizzy. The people who associated bubbles and fizz with beer, which was alcoholic, started to refer to Mr Codd's fizzy drinks as 'cods-wallop' because it was *not* alcoholic.

This gradually extended to meaning anything somewhat deceptive, not delivering what it promised, and eventually it came to mean anything that wasn't true or was just nonsense, a waste of time.

Q What is the origin of *cohort*?

Cohort is a word that has developed from a military term in Latin: *cohors* was a unit of infantry in an ancient Roman legion. Probably because the men all fought in a united cause, the English meaning developed, with a t: a group with the same purpose or having a common factor.

Q Why did they used to place *coins* on the eyes of dead people?

There has always been a widespread preference that dead people should have their eyes closed, but it doesn't always happen like this — and even when a person dies with their eyes closed, the eyelids sometimes ease open later quite unexpectedly.

So from time immemorial, people closed the deceased's eyes with their fingertips, and put coins on the lids to hold the eyes closed until after rigor mortis set in.

In some Asian religions coins are distributed at a funeral, and the ancient Greeks used to put a coin in a dead person's mouth, to pay their way into the next world. But in what is loosely called 'Western' tradition, coins were placed on the eyelids simply because they were an appropriate shape and weight, and were generally conveniently found in a household.

The practice isn't all that common today, maybe because undertakers can now travel to a death more quickly, but as recently as 1996 a New Zealand family put coins on their dead father's eyes to hold them closed until the undertaker arrived.

Modern undertakers have access to a discreet little plastic catch that can hold eyes closed even if they originally weren't, because the basic principle behind the custom still applies: people prefer that a dead person has closed eyes.

Does *college* mean a tertiary institution and, if so, why are so many secondary schools in New Zealand called colleges?

In strict dictionary terms the meaning of college is an institute of higher learning, usually part of a university.

But, over time, words develop different meanings and the word *college* has been used in New Zealand for some years to describe secondary schools. It may be some form of snobbery to make things sound better than they are. The same attitude has crept in with the constant reference to schoolchildren as students instead of pupils. In general, student used to mean someone who studies, and pupil used to mean someone who is taught by a teacher. Nowadays, they're all referred to as students, even when they're eight years old. The word pupil has gone out of fashion and seems to be used by the media only when someone has done something wrong.

 Why do we get the *collywobbles* when we're nervous?

The word has been around since the 18th century, and although it's not absolutely certain, most sources believe that it is related to colic, which is a painful condition named originally from the word colon, where the abdominal trouble stems from.

The *Oxford Dictionary* makes the strong suggestion that the word collywobbles is actually an evolved combination of the word colic, meaning trouble in the stomach, with wobbles, meaning general disorientation. So it's not just a painful stomach, like colic, but a general feeling of unease, usually nervousness, or diarrhoea.

Q What is the origin of *to come a cropper*?

This expression refers to birds. Originally, come a cropper didn't actually mean anything to do with falling; it was to do with failing, and failing badly and completely.

The crop is the business part of a bird's digestion, and a very old expression, neck and crop, meant fully and completely, and was often used to describe a complete failure. Gradually that became modified to simply cropper then to come a cropper, which still means completely but with the added connotation of failure. Nowadays it is also used to describe an actual fall.

But coming a cropper originated with the image of a bird having its neck and crop lopped off. After all, if a bird has no neck or crop, it is very definitely a failed bird, an ex-parrot.

The word *contumely* looks like an adverb, but is actually a noun. How has that happened?

Contumely is a noun that means lies or invective. Normally English words ending with *ly* are adverbs — they add to a verb, e.g. she walked slowly, he ate ravenously, etc.

But this word is derived from the Latin noun *contumelia* which itself is related to the Latin *tumere*, to swell (as in tumescence). *Contumelia* in Latin meant insulting language, scornful rudeness, disgrace and ignominy — and was a noun. This gravitated into English with its final a changed into a *y*, so it looks the same as English adverbs, but isn't one.

What is the origin of *couch potato*?

When television became popular, Americans created a slang term for it: the boob tube. This term was never used in Britain, where boob tube meant a tight, knitted top. (Americans don't like being reminded that television is a British invention.) People who watched a lot of television became boob tubers.

Then some bright cartoonist published a sketch showing a well-known kind of tuber, a potato, sitting on a sofa watching TV. As a kind of joke, the expression couch potato caught on.

But this was only fairly recently; the protocol of language decrees that a new word isn't taken seriously until it has been printed in something and published. The first known printing of the term couch potato was 1976.

Q **Is *coward* a shortened version of *cow-herd*?**

No, it's a different word altogether. Coward is derived from an Old French word *cuard*, which was borrowed even further back from the Latin *cauda*, meaning tail. The word coward is generally used about someone scared of danger or pain or difficulty — and it is thought that the Latin word for tail was applied because such a person is like an animal with its tail between its legs.

Q **Why is *cricket* so called?**

The English language has two crickets and it used to have three.

First there is the insect, a cricket, whose name comes from an ancient French word meaning to creak, and a slightly more modern Dutch word, *krekel*. Both are imitative of the noise a cricket makes. Then there is the game of cricket, and its name is also French, from the word *criquet*, meaning a post or wicket. Three hundred years ago, another word cricket in English meant a three-legged stool.

It's a coincidence — scholars seem to agree that the game of cricket is named not after that stool, but after French posts.

Q **Is *crikey* an English version of the Maori word *Karaiti*, which itself is a Maori version of the English word *Christ*?**

The short answer is no. Crikey is recognised in English as a euphemism for Christ and the word has been well established for a long time. The Maori word Karaiti, on the other hand, is a transliteration of the word Christ, which is quite a different thing.

It's not totally impossible that a Maori influence crept in, but it seems unlikely because the word crikey was known in England when New Zealand was still just an emerging nation.

Incidentally, Christ is not an English word: it's Greek for 'the anointed one'. Greek translators put it next to the name Jesus to indicate status; Christ is not Jesus's second name and never was.

 Why does *I'm crook* mean I'm ill?

In New Zealand to *be* crook means that a person or a thing is ill, sick or somehow disabled, and to *go* crook means to get angry. Crook in these senses seems to be Australian in origin, since in Britain crook means a curved shepherd's stick or a criminal. Crook meaning ill has been in use in New Zealand since the early part of this century. The word originates from an old German word meaning hook or caught on a hook.

I don't know of any explanation as to why Australasians say they're crook when they're sick, but I'll stick my neck out and give a personal opinion. All the meanings we've mentioned do relate back to being bent out of line — like a shepherd's crook, a person whose morals are crooked and commits deliberate crime, or a person who is suffering a curve away from their normal good health. In an odd kind of way, all those things could be called crook, which is usually short for crooked.

 Is the name for the game *croquet* related in any way to the craft of *crochet*?

Yes, there is a link between crochet and croquet, but it's a bit complex. There are two different things going on here: the origin of the game, and the origin of the name.

The game we call croquet actually originates in an Italian game, *palla maglio*, meaning to hit a ball with a mallet. From that Italian term came two English expressions: first, pell mell meaning to rush about, and, second, because the game *palla maglio* was often played in a certain London street, that street became known as Pall Mall, a long avenue. From that came the modern word mall usually meaning a collection of shops where you walk and there's no traffic.

In the meantime, the actual game of *palla maglio* took on a new name, based on the French word for hook, *crotchet*. In modern English, the French word has three descendants: (1) crochet is a kind of embroidery done with a hook, (2) crotchet is the name of a musical note, shaped something like a crook, and (3) the game formerly known as *palla maglio* slowly became called croquet because, apparently, the very early versions of the game did have a hooked mallet for hitting the ball.

Q What is the origin of *I'll crown you*?

Crown you has been in use since the 12th century to mean hitting over the head, as well as a genuine crowning. The context in which the expression appears is supposed to indicate the correct meaning.

Q Why is a thing like a *curate's egg* when it is only good in parts?

The curate's egg, which was good only in parts, dates back to a famous 1895 cartoon by George Du Maurier in the magazine *Punch*. The cartoon, titled 'True Humility', showed a bishop exclaiming to his curate, 'I'm afraid you have a bad egg.' The curate was replying bravely, 'Oh no, my lord, parts of it are excellent.'

This latter clause has been contracted over the years into the vernacular 'good in parts'. The original cartoon still survives.

Why, when sports stadiums have no curtain, are warm-up games described as *curtain raisers*?

The origins of the term lie in the French theatre, where a little event in front of the curtain before the main show was called a *lever de rideau*. Now the expression is applied to anything preliminary to a bigger happening, whether there's a curtain or not.

 When something goes wrong and turns into a disaster, why do people say *it turned to custard*?

Custard by its very nature is formless, shapeless, and difficult to control. Custard's best friend could not call it structured and organised. Much as we enjoy it, it's a bit of a mess.

 In the expression *He took off like a cut cat*, does cut mean drunk?

There are at least 12 different meanings of the word cut and one of these is to move fast, as in 'he cut down a side street', but I can't find any reference to cut and cat being put together with specifically that meaning.

Cut also can mean drunk — 'He went out last night and got properly cut' — but again it doesn't seem to match up with a cat moving quickly.

In New Zealand cut also means castrated, and I have the impression that cut cat is an all-Kiwi expression, meaning moving away rapidly from a recent disaster — like a cat that's just been castrated.

D

Q How did the *D-Day* of the Normandy landings in 1944 get its name?

The usual explanation is that D is just an abbreviation of day, a sort of alliteration, but in 1964 General Eisenhower was asked for an explanation and his letter of reply said that any amphibious operation has a departed date, and D simply stood for departed.

Since the Second World War the use of the expression has been broadened a great deal to mean a specific date for a planned event, or a deadline.

Q Why do we call someone *a bit of a dag*?

Dag has two separate derivations.

In English, for over 300 years, the word dag has meant a loose, hanging bit of something, and it was even used to describe a skirt or jacket with a pointy hem — 'Your new sleeves look lovely with their dag hem'. There's a possible relationship with the word tag, which also meant a small strip of something — for example, a price tag. When the word dag was first used to mean the lump of rubbish hanging off the back of a sheep it was called a dag-lock and in time that was shortened to just dag.

Dag meaning hard case, a lively fellow, is a different word altogether, also about 300 years old. Some people think it is a relative of the word wag but scholars reveal that, in the 17th century, an artful or impudent fellow was called a degen, which is a kind of sword. So if you said the word about a person it meant he was knowing blade, or was willing to be daring. Degen eventually became contracted to dag.

Rattle your dags, meaning to move fast, probably derives quite simply from sheep running — when they do so their dags rattle.

 Q **Why do New Zealanders usually call their corner store a *dairy*?**

It's an example of usage that has broadened over the years from an original fact. In 1908 the law of New Zealand stated that a licence issued to a shop called a dairy meant it could only sell milk, eggs and perishable dairy products such as butter.

At that part of the 20th century there was no refrigeration and nearly all shops closed over the weekend but since dairy produce in general was very perishable and had to be bought fresh, the licensed dairies were allowed to be open at weekends, and gradually they started to stock other things.

Although the name dairy stuck around, other terms have also been used. Cash grocer was one, and at one time they were widely referred to as lolly shops. Corner shop or corner store are frequent nowadays, but the term dairy still remains.

These kind of mixed shops are quite common around the world but each culture has a different name for them: in Italy they're called a salt and tobacco shop, and Americans call them a drugstore or a liquor store.

 Q **What do people mean when they say *I got my dander up*?**

One writer put forward the theory that because angry people clutch at their hair, it could be a shortened version of getting your dandruff up or, rather, bringing it down, but this isn't the case.

The expression is believed to be of mid-19th-century American origin. At that time many immigrants to the United States were Dutch or German. The German word for thunder is *Donner* and the Dutch word is *Donder*, so etymologists think it arose as a misuse by other Americans when they heard such settlers using *Donder*, in particular, to mean anger. So eventually the word crept into a phrase, the rest of which was in English, and people got their dander up.

 Why is the place in a car where all the dials are called the *dashboard*?

The word is over 100 years old and dates back to the days of carriages when there was an upright board near the front to prevent splashings of water and mud onto the drivers and passengers. A similar protection board, with the same name, was also used on boats.

When cars and aircraft were invented, they were fairly open and also needed a protection sheet, which was called the dashboard. Over the years vehicles became more enclosed, and their dials and instruments, by logic, were situated on a panel in front of the driver. The word remained, but now when we say dashboard, we don't mean that it keeps the rain, wind, mud and spray away; it is the nerve centre of the vehicle's control.

 What does *dead reckoning* mean?

This is a nautical expression for 'calculating a ship's position by plotting on from the last fix or observed position, the speed made good through the water along the compass course steered', to quote *Brewer's Dictionary of Phrase and Fable*.

 When you say *deal to*, shouldn't that mean only cards?

It used to mean only giving out cards. But now deal *to* instead of deal *with* seems to be a new use of words, because deal *to* doesn't mean giving out cards and it doesn't mean the same as deal with.

To deal *with* means to treat a particular subject ('this book deals with . . .') or to be active and to cope ('to deal with a difficult situation'). But deal *to* has come to mean to effect retribution, or take action against.

Unlike meet with or visit with, where the extra word is unnecessary, deal to has evolved as a new expression slightly different from deal with and is now used very widely.

Q **What is the correct meaning of *decimate*?**

The correct and original meaning was to destroy every tenth one. But gradually it has come to mean just general destruction, and when you hear that a cyclone has decimated farmers' crops, it isn't intended to mean that the cyclone mowed down just one plant in every ten. It's intended to mean that the whole lot or a majority of plants were destroyed.

Q **Is it valid for a *dentist* to be referred to as doctor?**

There are three different factors to consider here. First, there's university protocol. In general, university qualifications are ranked; they usually begin with the qualification of diploma, the next one up is a bachelor degree, then comes the master's degree, and finally, after many years of work and effort, there might come a doctorate. Strictly speaking, only a person holding a doctorate degree should be addressed as Dr so-and-so.

But the word doctor has acquired another meaning: a person who is qualified to practise medicine. People who legally practise medicine very often have a bachelor medical degree, but they are customarily referred to as doctors. Dentists who study just as assiduously and just as long as medical students also emerge with a bachelor degree — a BDS. (There is a doctorate degree in dentistry but it isn't found very frequently.)

In the United States, dentists who graduate at the same level as New Zealand dental graduates are immediately granted a DDS, which entitles them to be addressed as doctor.

Since the 1970s there has been an awareness that someone holding a New Zealand bachelor of dentistry has an equal level of skill to someone in the United States holding what *they* call a doctorate of dental surgery.

So by a kind of courtesy, and a form of linguistic osmosis, New Zealand dentists with a bachelor degree are frequently referred to by the same title as their American equivalents, and may be called Dr. There's nothing ominous or fraudulent about it — we all call our medical man or woman Dr so-and-so even if he or she, strictly speaking, holds a bachelor degree (in medicine).

Q Why did schoolboys used to shout out *Dickens*?

This has nothing to do with Charles Dickens. It's a word that has been around for years as a kind of substitute for saying the Devil. Shakespeare used the word in *The Merry Wives of Windsor* and it survives in such expressions as 'Where the dickens did I put that?' There are many variations in the word's use, and during the 1940s it was often used in New Zealand as an exclamation of surprise, with variations, especially among teenagers who would yell out Dickens when they meant cut out the rough stuff.

Q What is the meaning of the word *diddicai*?

Real gypsies are very protective about their bloodline and about who marries who. They're not keen about people marrying outside the gypsy fraternity, and they have some scorn for people who are not full-blooded gypsies but who follow a gypsy lifestyle.

Within the Romany language the word diddicai (there are several English versions) refers to *those* people, the ones who give every appearance of being gypsies, but are not the real thing. So diddicai is a gypsy word, used by gypsies, to describe someone who is *not* a real full-blooded gypsy.

Q **Is there a difference between *dilemma* and *problem*?**

Yes and no. Dilemma is a word used in the study of formal rhetoric, where it has a specific meaning, namely a form of argument wherein a choice between two or more alternatives is possible, but the alternatives are equally unfavourable.

But there is a human disease, found particularly in media, called Making Things Sound Grander Than They Are, and so dictionaries nowadays will note that the word dilemma is often used to describe a position of doubt or perplexity, a difficult situation.

So we have to accept that dilemma has undergone an expansion of meaning and can now be used without there being two equally unattractive results.

 Q **Why do crosswords sometimes give the clue underworld when the answer is *Dis*?**

Dis is from Latin and it comes sometimes with a capital letter and sometimes without. Dis with a small d in Latin means apart and has come into English meaning separated or reversed, as in disappear, disconnect and disembodied.

But when Dis has a capital letter in Latin it means the Roman god of the underworld, or the underworld itself. In Roman mythology the god is called either Dis or Pluto. In Greek mythology the underworld is called Hades.

Q **What does *discombobulating* mean and where does it come from?**

It has existed for nearly 100 years. Probably we don't hear the word too often because it is actually quite difficult to say — you have to be what is called orally confident. Discombobulate means disturbed, upset or, better, disconnected.

I've read it in descriptions of political campaigning: getting on and off a bus for speeches and photo opportunities without being sure what town they're in or what day it is makes candidates feel discombobulated.

The *Oxford Dictionary* doesn't know the exact derivation of the word but suggests that it is a deliberately doctored version of the older word 'discomposed', which has the right meaning, but rather a Jane Austen sound to it. Perhaps discombobulated has evolved because it sounds more novel and slightly more technological.

Q Why is a pretty girl often referred to as a *dish*?

The word dish is partly an interesting example of meaning reversal. Expressions sometimes do this: what used to be praised as hot, is now praised by calling it cool; bimbo actually means boy, but is used to mean girl; chuffed, which means pleased and lively, used to mean sour and morose.

When Shakespeare used the word dish about woman, it was admittedly only half the expression — he called an ugly woman a dish-clout. But a change came early this century and by about 1930 dish and dishy were commonly used by men to describe an attractive woman. The first known publication of the expression was in 1936.

It's an example of food imagery being used to refer to types of people, such as cheesecake, beefcake and probably hunk.

In more recent years the term dish has begun to be considered politically incorrect when referring to women, but it is now considered completely acceptable for women to say it about men!

Q Is there a masculine version of the word *diva*?

Linguistically, yes there probably is because diva comes ultimately from the Latin *divinus* meaning godly or divine; it's actually the feminine form of an Italian word, like *bambina*. I suppose you could say *divo* and it would become a masculine god, or a masculine opera star, but I've never heard anyone say that. It just isn't used.

A goddess, a diva, has two essential requirements: she must seem to be elevated from ordinary mortals, and she must have a following — there's no point in being a goddess if nobody takes any notice of you.

In earlier centuries, women opera stars were the megastars of their time. Dame Nellie Melba and Jenny Lind, for instance, were mega-mega-stars. Of course during those centuries, female opera singers were the only type of star there was — because they were the only ones you could hear. And they gradually began to be referred to as divas — elevated beyond the norm, and with huge numbers of fans.

The practice of referring to the really famous women of opera as divas remained in place until the invention of electricity. In the late 1920s, when the microphone started to be used, gradually there came radio, a recording industry and then sound movies and television — and gradually it became possible for women with tiny voices also to become elevated beyond the norm and to gain followings. So, very tentatively at first, the word diva was occasionally also used for the other kind of star — the electricity star.

The word diva is still most effective when used about famous women singers, though occasionally you hear the description diva for a person who is a non-singer.

Curiously, the word is never commonly used in the male version. There have been many famous male singers with microphone and without — Caruso, Gigli, Sinatra, Crosby, Pavarotti, Robbie Williams — but I've never heard them referred to as divos. It's the same with the other opera expression *prima donna* or first lady: you never say *primo uomo* for a leading man. Ballerina, too, has no easy male equivalent.

The use of the female version of diva is so old that it is actually part of the historic relationship between male and female. In the days when goddesses were genuinely worshipped, the social position of women in general was fairly suffocated. So at least among women there was a greater attraction in paying attention to *female* goddesses than to male ones, partly because these were feminine figures with charisma and power, and that didn't happen so much in real life.

It was the same with the famous women singers: they had marvellous voices, their performances transcended all the male/female rules of power and they caused admiration — and yet they were real. And throughout the ages the most famous opera and ballet stars have been women — there have been only a handful of men.

 Where does the word *doff* come from, as in doff one's hat?

Ancient Assyria, which stretched from Egypt to Iran, required all military captives to strip nude in order to demonstrate subjugation, and the ancient Greeks required all new servants to strip from the waist up. Gradually there evolved the idea of taking off an article of clothing to demonstrate respect. Ancient Romans took their sandals off before approaching a holy shrine and taking shoes off to demonstrate respect still survives in several cultures today, e.g. Japanese and Maori.

In Europe, by the time of the Middle Ages, inferior social status was shown by the person of lower rank taking off their hat when a person of superior rank was present. This action said, in effect, 'I am your servant'. The custom survives in the Christian church where men are expected to take their hats off because they are in the presence of a greater power.

Outside the church, taking hats right off continued as an acknowledgement to a person of superior rank — or in the presence of that universally greater power called woman. This dwindled eventually into simply touching the hat.

Doff = do + off (and the opposite is don = do + on). The do is as in do out, do down, do in, do over, do up, do without.

 Why is *dog* also used to describe some women?

This seems to be an entirely American usage. Various dog expressions have been used for centuries to downgrade men, usually mongrel or cur, and by 1700 the word dog was being attached to expressions that meant low-rated things — doghouse, dog's breakfast, dog Latin.

But there's a contradiction, because round about 300 years ago the word dog was also used to mean a rakish, lively man — usually with an adjective like lucky dog, jovial dog, sly old dog.

The word was widely used in the United States to describe something poor or mediocre, e.g. 'I made a financial investment which turned out to be a dog.' Since about 1930 that meaning extended to include certain women. *Webster's American Dictionary* says a dog is a woman inferior in looks or character.

 Why do people sometimes refer to Port Chalmers as *Dog Town*?

There are two explanations for the term Dog Town. The first has its clue in the name of the town, Port Chalmers, which obviously had a lot of docks. As with the Isle of Dogs in London, there is a belief that in the old days the docks of Port Chalmers caused it to be referred to as Dock Town, and the word became corrupted.

But there are also legends that, again because of the town's shipping orientation, there were always many seamen about, sometimes unemployed, and all of them were accompanied by their dogs. Most of these men lived in cottages in George Street which became known locally as Dog Town and the name spread to mean Port Chalmers in general. It's occasionally heard even today.

 What is the origin of *dogsbody*?

The word is believed to originate in the Navy (as many colourful expressions do). If you take a lot of dried peas and boil them up in a cloth for several hours, you get a pease pudding, a messy kind of lump that used to be served in the Navy. It was very nutritious but the men said it looked like the cooked body of a dog.

By the early 20th century this pudding word had become a pejorative term for a lowly person, a drudge who carries out menial tasks for others. Lawrence of Arabia used the term — 'I'll get used to being a dogsbody' — in 1922.

 Why does the *dollar sign* sometimes have two vertical lines through it but usually only one?

The word dollar comes originally from Czechoslovakia — *Joachims-tal*, tal meaning valley. Eventually this became *thaler* in several languages and in English became dollar.

The dollar sign is related to a very old Spanish sign for *pesos* which is believed to be a symbolic depiction of the pillars of Hercules with a scroll wrapped around them. But that scroll could also have been a distorted figure eight, because that coin was worth one-eighth of a Spanish real — hence the expression pieces of eight, meaning gold coins of smallish denomination.

As usual, there is some confusion about how the sign became established in the United States and how it changed. The word was first used in the States in 1683, and Thomas Jefferson wrote a memo with the dollar sign in it in 1784 — he put two vertical strokes, which was the norm at that time.

Later there were many Americans who liked those two vertical strokes to be joined up like a letter U — when you put that over the S shape, to an imaginative person it says US. Decimal dollar currency was formally adopted in America in 1785 (as opposed to adopting the British system which the settlers had been used to back home) and the two vertical lines remained for some time.

Q **Can polite people use the term *donkey deep*?**

It seems, although they are quite smallish creatures, male donkeys in particular are not small in all their components. And as someone with a naval background explained to me, with supreme diplomacy, male donkeys are 'enthusiastic and skilful opponents of birth control'. It would seem therefore that whatever other derivations the phrase donkey deep has, according to etymologists, male donkeys with only one thing in mind can display a distinct potency that gives the expression a particularly physical connotation.

 Where does the word *dope* originate?

Dope comes from the Dutch word *doop* meaning a sauce, to dip, mix or add to. It drifted into English and was used to mean the liquid applied to fabric on early aeroplanes. But, as some people know, when you cook up opium, it also starts out as a thick sticky liquid, and this rather treacly commodity began to be referred to as dope because it was rather like the goo used on plane fabrics.

This secondary meaning gradually came to refer to any form of narcotic, whether it was stimulating or stupefying and whether it was liquid, powder, solid or even smoke. From there came the word dopey — for a person influenced by drugs and eventually a person acting as if he or she were influenced by drugs.

And because the dope used on aeroplane fabrics was also an additive, the silicon chip industry uses the word when they deliberately add any kind of impurity to a computer chip to make it act a certain way.

Q Is there a connection between *dope* and the words *dozy*, *dippy* and *drippy*?

No. Dopey does come from dope, but dozy obviously comes from doze, and therefore has a different origin, although it does also mean sleepy and slow.

Dippy and drippy both seem to have the same ancestor in the Old English *dyppan*, to let down into a liquid briefly. It is sometimes used to describe a person, presumably to mean that they haven't been properly immersed in something (like good sense) and intelligence comes off them only in small *drips*.

So there you have dope, dopey, dozy, dippy and drippy — a good name for a pop group.

 What is the meaning of the word *doryphore*?

This ancient Greek word meaning spear carrier was attached by an etymologist to a beetle he'd discovered, which presumably looked as if it were carrying a spear. And then, by a process of evolution, it has become a word you can say about nasty critics — possibly because they carry a spear and are always ready to strike at public performers.

Q **Why is a *drawing room* so called? Does it mean that the family went there to do their sketching and drawing?**

The word dates from a time when, in the moneyed classes, women were expected to be separated from men at certain times of the social day, especially after dinner. So the men would stay at the table drinking port, and the women would withdraw — to the withdrawing room. In time, for convenience, the word became shorter, just as omnibus became bus and taxi cabriolet became taxi or cab.

So the withdrawing room eventually was called just the drawing room, and although the notion of withdrawing slipped away, the room itself retained a certain image of behaving properly. Then it became known as the sitting room, before it relaxed a bit further and is now often called the lounge or living room.

Why do we say someone is *dressed to the nines*?

Some people think it refers to the 99th Regiment of Foot, who were notable for their splendid uniforms. Others think it refers to a scale of values where 10 is the top so 9 means you've dressed with considerable effort.

But the main opinion is that the expression is much older than that. In ye olden times the word 'eye' was singular, as it is now, but the plural used to be *eyne* (not eyes) and it is believed that dressed to the nines was once dressed to the eyne, making yourself look as good as possible, wearing everything, pleasing for other people to see.

Q **People who write and speak about cooking constantly use the word *drizzle*. Has this word changed its meaning?**

Yes and no. Drizzle means light rain falling in small drops, specifically drops that are less than half a millimetre in diameter. It still means that. Given the viscosity of oil at room temperature, people who talk about drizzling oil must surely be dealing in drops larger than that. Wouldn't it be more appropriate to use the correct word, dribble?

I suspect that people resist the word dribble because it has other connotations, and they've simply taken up saying drizzle because it sounds cute. So the short answer is that when they say drizzle they mean dribble. If the fluid is pumped in fine drops out of a machine, then it is neither a dribble nor a drizzle but a *spray*.

But usage often dictates language growth, and I suspect that soon we will find that dictionaries say drizzle means light rain in very small drops, *or* to moisten food from above by the method formerly known as dribbling.

Why is a cricketer out for a *duck*?

This is fairly straightforward. Cricket usually has a visual scoreboard, and if a player leaves the field having made no runs, a great big nought stands next to his or her name on the board. A practice arose many years ago of referring to this as a duck's egg, and this has shortened to just a duck. So if he or she was out for a duck, it means that the score was zero.

There is a similar development with the tennis score called love, which also means zero. The term originated in France, and when the player scored zero and that appeared on the board, the French thought exactly the same as the English — that it looked like an egg. So the French said a person's score was *l'oeuf* — an egg. English people began to say it too but got it slightly wrong: *l'oeuf* became pronounced as love and for the last 250 years, that's the word the English language has used for a zero score in tennis.

 Where does *duck shove*, meaning to avoid something or not take responsibility, come from?

Ducks do shove each other out of the way, of course, but Kiwi slang expert David McGill believes that this particular meaning originated in Australia about 1900 when taxi drivers in Melbourne jumped the queue for customers, not putting their taxis at the end of the line as they came in. The other drivers called them duck-shovers because, by not taking their proper place, they were not playing fair and were avoiding a long wait.

Q **Why are there so many expressions in English that include the word *Dutch*?**

English, meaning English as spoken in Britain, is alarmingly non-PC about its references to foreigners. Just watch Benny Hill or *Fawlty Towers* and see how bold they are on the subject.

There are over 30 expressions in English that use the word

Dutch, usually as some kind of put-down or joke. For instance, calling one's wife my old Dutch means she has a funny face like a Dutch clock and saying someone is like a Dutch uncle means they are severe, because the British think the Dutch are very disciplined and organised.

The expression talking double Dutch started out in the mid-19th century as Dutch talk, meaning foreigners speaking a language the British couldn't understand, and because Holland was a close foreign country the word Dutch was used simply to mean foreign. It slowly modified into the expression double Dutch and the meaning extended to include not just foreign languages, but technical talk and gobbledygook (such as computer or political jargon) that ordinary people can't understand.

Going Dutch — or Dutch shout or Dutch treat — started out as Dutch treat in the 1870s, meaning that everyone pays for themselves. New Zealand prefers the word *shout* but it means the same thing and is based on the vague perception that Dutch people are frugal and well organised financially.

Dutch courage has been used since the 18th century. It's believed to have originated because the British thought the Dutch were heavy drinkers, and so Dutch courage is a temporary sham bravery brought on by having had sufficient strong drink to blot out reality.

 What is the origin of the word *dysfunctional*?

The prefix *dys*, which crops up occasionally in English, is Greek and means bad, difficult, abnormal or faulty. Originally it was used in various medical terms in English, to indicate that whatever word came after it was not in good working order. So dysentery is a malfunction of the enteric or intestine system, dyslexia is the inability to recognise whole words and dyspepsia is an upset stomach and digestion. Gradually the prefix crept into more general use, so dysfunction isn't too much of a shock.

There is also a move towards spelling the *dys* as *dis*, because people can't be bothered putting the *y*. But I think this could muddy up the meanings, because where *dys* indicates that something bad is afoot, *dis* indicates an opposite condition, as in like/dislike, agree/disagree.

So at the moment if you spell it *dys*functional you mean things are going badly but they're still lumping along, but if you spell it *dis*functional you mean that things have stopped working altogether.

New Zealanders often say *eck-setera*. Is this correct?

Certainly not. The phrase is Latin for and the other things and it must be said et cetera. Reversing the order of the letters and putting the c before the t just doesn't make sense and is wrong, lazy and stupid.

This is an example of a strange New Zealand habit of putting things back to front, as in aks for ask, and vunlerable for vulnerable.

 How did the London suburb called *Elephant and Castle* get its name?

The usual legend is that the expression originated from the inability of Cockney Londoners to pronounce the title of the king's wife, Eleanor of Castile, who was a Spanish princess and therefore correctly called Infanta de Castile. But that king was Edward I in the 13th century, so it's a bit difficult to verify.

There's another version, that for many years trained elephants have carried a little box up on their backs, called a howdah, in which nobles sat, or sometimes people armed for battle. This was referred to as the castle on the elephant and could possibly have been the origin of the sign outside the pub in Newington Butts which is the source of the legend.

 Did Bruce Mason create the phrase *The End of the Golden Weather*?

In New Zealand, it's known as the name of a famous one-man

play, written and performed by the late Dr Bruce Mason. He first performed it in 1959 and then went on performing it for 19 years all over New Zealand. Such was its popularity that he often performed it in little towns that didn't have a hall. Then he took it to the Edinburgh Festival and then back throughout New Zealand again several times. It was made into a TV special and he rewrote it into a full-cast play and then it was made into a full-length movie.

But Mason didn't create the title. It's a quotation from an American novel published in 1941, *The Web and the Rock* by Thomas Clayton Wolfe. But say the phrase anywhere in New Zealand and people will immediately respond — Bruce Mason.

 What's the difference between the *evil eye* and a *roving eye*?

A roving eye describes a person who has a lively interest in successive members of the opposite sex.

The evil eye is rather more ominous. For many centuries there was a strong belief that certain powerful people possessed an evil eye that could kill with a glance or blight crops or cause impotence or be responsible for such disabilities as blindness or deformity. One mythical Celtic king in Ireland had the gift so powerfully that when his eyelid was lifted in death, those who saw the dead eye died.

It was sometimes creatures who had the power, like the legends of the Gorgon, or the basilisk (a kind of serpent). Some people think that peacock feathers contain a depiction of the evil eye, and won't have them in the house.

Q **Does *fail-safe* mean the same thing as *foolproof*?**

It's a complete misuse of fail-safe when you mean something that won't go wrong — that's foolproof. Fail-safe means something that is able to return to a stable condition after a malfunction. In other words, if it fails, it fails in a safe way.

Q **What did Andy Warhol actually say about being *famous*?**

It was first published in Stockholm in 1968 and what he wrote was, 'In the future, everyone will be world famous for fifteen minutes'.

Q **How did *fay nits* arise?**

It's a fairly rare survival of a very old word indeed; in fact, it hasn't really survived at all. We're speaking about the word fain, which is a very old way of saying willing and is heard in such archaic structures as 'She fain would be dead' meaning she'd prefer to be dead, or is willing to die.

Fay nits was an expression that grew from this, originally to end an argument by saying fain I was to call a truce — I'm willing to cease hostilities.

The fain I was corrupted into fay nits with crossed fingers as some extra sort of submission symbol, and that was the sign for a truce or some kind of withdrawal. Paradoxically, the expression also occasionally meant the opposite and became a statement of opposition or irony: I'm willing to believe you, but I don't really.

Q **Why are *Filipinos* spelt with an F when their country is spelt Philippines?**

Portuguese navigator Ferdinand Magellan arrived in the Phillipines in 1521 and named the country as Saint Lazarus.

Some years later, the country was renamed after the future king of Spain, Philip II, then only 16. It was then spelt with an F, as the King's name was: Felipe is Spanish for Philip. But when the country was referred to by English-speaking people, they spelt it with Ph because that's how Philip is spelt in English.

However, we seem to have retained some tribute to the Spanish king, and we spell the inhabitants Filipinas or Filipinos.

Q **Where does the phrase *in fine fettle* come from?**

Fettling is the cleaning up of pieces that have just been cast in iron, scraping off any little flecks and so on; when you've finished, the piece is looking fine because it has been fettled.

Fetel is a very old English word for girdle or belt, so when you were dressed and then held together with a good belt or *fetel*, you were *in fine fetel* (with one t) which became fettle with two ts.

It appears that the iron foundry expression also derives from the same source: when a new piece has all its irregularities removed, it has been fettled and thus is wearing its best belt.

The word fetlock is different altogether. The *fet* in fetlock comes from Middle High German *vizzel*, which is that part of a horse's leg.

Q **What is the origin of the phrase *of the first water*?**

Of the first water comes from an expression used in classifying diamonds. The quality of the stone is described as its water and of the first water means it's a stone of the finest kind. Diamonds sometimes have visible imperfections that can't be disguised by cutting, so one could guess that if the stone were absolutely clear, then this might be the reason for saying it was as clear as water. A totally clear stone with no coloration would be first water and so on — though one never hears about anything being of the second or third water.

Diamond comes from the old Greek word *adamas*, meaning invincible, hard. It came into English through a Latin adaptation and was corrupted into the English word diamond. But the Greek still occurs in adamant — unyielding.

Q **Why do we say that someone yells *like a fishwife*?**

This dates from long-ago days when the word *wif* simply meant woman. In the coastal towns the men went out and caught fish and the women sold it, often in the open air. This was extremely competitive and the women selling fish were known for a strident style of voice and a fierce flow of invective, sometimes against each other. This element of scolding and using a rather coarse vocal style eventually broadened its application and is sometimes applied to women whose use of voice is less than attractive. (Critics said it about Elizabeth Taylor after her movie *Cleopatra*.)

Q **What is the origin of the expression *to fit the bill*?**

The real original expression might well have been fill the bill and it's been corrupted over the years to fit the bill. They both mean the same thing — to be suitable, right for the purpose — and have the same derivation.

The origin is an old theatrical term referring to the size of lettering used for a performer's name on the bill or poster. If the printing type was all laid out and then one actor had to drop out, the new actor who replaced him should ideally have exactly the same number of letters in his name, so that the type took up the same space — and filled, or fitted, the bill.

What is the origin of the term *flat stick*?

There are 38 separate meanings of the word flat and one of those is level, not displaying any angle. Flat stick means travelling as fast as possible or making the maximum effort.

Expressions closely related to this are flat tack, flat out and flat to the boards. The general consensus is that these probably originated from the fact that the accelerator of a car is normally set at an angle, but when it is pushed hard, it is flat and parallel to the floor of the vehicle — hence flat, meaning fast. Flat stick first appeared in print in New Zealand in the early 1970s.

Someone who has had a great deal to do with horses says that the expression flat stick is also used to refer to the whip used by riders. Presumably when the whip is upright it isn't being used, but if it is generally in the horizontal (or flat) position then the horse is being spurred to go faster.

Q **Should it be *flautist* or *flutist*?**

In the field of music, there are many discrepancies of language, particularly with words of foreign origin being used alongside English words. One of those discrepancies concerns the flute. Most players of instruments are described simply by modifying the name of the instrument — a clarinet is played by a clarinettist, a violin by a violinist, a bassoon by a bassoonist, etc. The flute, which is an Anglicised word, somehow escaped the system, and the person who played it was called a flautist, which is a version of the Italian word *flautista*.

Musicians in the United States began to rumble that it was ridiculous to single out one instrument and call its player by a foreign word when the others don't, and so started the new practice of calling a flute player a flutist.

Q **What ever is *floccinaucinihilipilification*?**

The word does exist: it means the habit of estimating almost everything as worthless. (It could be said perhaps about tabloid-style reporters.) In rarity of use the word is somewhat akin to solipsistic (the theory that the self is the only thing that actually exists). David Lange is the only person in the world who can use either of those two words and make them sound completely valid.

Q **Why is a servant sometimes called a *flunky*?**

First of all you have to imagine one of those very important people who are always seen with an equerry or assistant standing on each side of them. These attendants to VIPs are referred to as flankers, and that is believed to be the origin of the word flunky.

This kind of servant, the flanker, was usually dressed in the uniform (livery) that designated the master's rank, and about 200 years ago the word flunky evolved to mean anyone in livery, a servant.

Again we look to the Navy, where the word flunky was first noticed in common usage: it meant a wardroom attendant.

From its use in the Navy there evolved a more general meaning for flunky — of someone rather parasitic and toadying, a person of low rank who was associated with people of high rank, but in a menial capacity.

There's another similar word, to flunk, meaning to fail, which is rather more mysterious. It is believed to be derived from flinch, to recoil from something or avoid contact.

But the two words, flunky and flunk, have quite different ancestry and don't seem to have any historical connection.

Q **Why was a British whaler captain killed for his *flushing*?**

When Captain Cherry, master of the whaling ship *Caroline*, was murdered at Mana, near Wellington, it was thought he was killed merely for the sake of his clothes, a new suit of flushing.

Flushing was a name used many decades ago to describe a particular kind of woven woollen cloth; it no longer seems to be around. There can, however, be only a certain number of ways of weaving wool so it wouldn't surprise me if the same fabric is still among us but is called something else.

 Why is a certain size of paper called *foolscap*?

Because foolscap paper is quite big and you can make a dunce's hat out of it many people assume that's how the paper gets its name. But in fact it's all to do with one of the most successful paper manufacturers in Britain, a Mr Spielmann.

Because Spielmann is German for an actor, a showy person, Mr Spielmann used a picture of a jester in a cap as the watermark on his paper. That image became so associated in people's minds with the size of this paper that they eventually referred to it as foolscap.

There is an alternative version — that Oliver Cromwell, in dealing with official papers of the realm, took the royal crown off the letterhead and replaced it with a jester — but that story doesn't seem to be proven.

Why is a gay man sometimes referred to as *a friend of Dorothy's*?

The usual explanation for this expression is that in 1900 L. Frank Baum wrote a book called *The Wonderful Wizard of Oz*. It was made into a film, *The Wizard of Oz*, in 1939 starring Judy Garland in the role of the young girl Dorothy who had some rather wacky, eccentric misfit friends — a scarecrow, a tin man and a cowardly lion.

Garland became very famous and she had many personal problems, all of which the public got to hear about, and in her concerts she displayed an extraordinary vulnerability that appealed to the public in general and to gay people in particular. They couldn't say they were a friend of Judy Garland's because they didn't actually know her personally, so somehow the liking for her was described as being a friend of Dorothy's, which carried a connotation of being a slightly off-beat character. And eventually the phrase friend of Dorothy's narrowed down to mean gay people who admired Judy Garland and then, long after she was gone, just gay people.

Q **What is the origin of *funk* and *funky*?**

Funk has two meanings. In Britain the word has been used since the 18th century to mean scared, shrinking from — to be in a funk. But it has developed another shade of meaning in the United States — a strong smell — and since the late 1950s this term has been used to describe a certain type of music. It is funky, meaning earthy and rough.

After that, Americans widened the term to include people, clothes and furnishings, and eventually it has come to mean fashionable and a bit cheeky.

G

Q **Why is a skimpy piece of underwear often called a *G-string*?**

There are two possibilities: G is the lowest string on a violin, and a G-string is usually worn very low. But most scholars think it is a Native American word. When Europeans first met the people they called Red Indians, the men wore a little loin cloth known in their native language as a *gee*.

There is also some belief that because of what a G-string usually covers, the G stands for genital.

Q **What is the origin of *galleyed*?**

Galley is a term of the old printing trade, referring to the tray that held the metal type.

Galley was also once a kind of ship, working in which was very hard, so a person who was galleyed was overworked, a drudge, a galley slave. In more recent times the word galley is used only to describe the ship's kitchen, which may be hot and crowded, so being on duty there is also liable to make a person overworked.

But galleyed can also mean uncertain or wavering and this is probably a different matter altogether. There is an old dialect word gally, meaning to frighten, or to vex, so to be galleyed can mean fatigued with worry or uncertain.

Q **What is the difference between *gamut* and *gambit*?**

Gamut was the lowest note in a musical scale, usually the bottom G on the bottom line of the stave. Its meaning widened to refer to the whole musical scale, and has now extended to mean the whole range of anything, usually emotions.

Gambit comes from the Italian *gambetto*, meaning to trip up. The term is often used in chess. A gambit is a manoeuvre intended to gain some advantage, and it has come to mean the proposing of a certain point of view — to persuade people to think something is advantageous.

Q **What are *gandy dancers*?**

They are the builders of, and maintenance people on, American railway trains. The expression is thought to have come from the fact that in the 19th century there was a large engineering firm in Chicago called the Gandy Manufacturing Company, which made many of the parts used in trains.

Workers who tapped ballast underneath the sleepers with a spade or shovel had a particularly vigorous and active job, and it is believed that they were referred to as gandy dancers. From there, it extended to mean all the people who unpacked the parts and worked on the trains.

Q **Do throwing down and running the *gauntlet* have the same origin?**

This is one of those awkward situations where the English language has acquired a word that is actually two words with two quite separate origins.

Gauntlet No. 1 derives from a Germanic word *gant*, meaning glove. This gives us gauntlet meaning a leather glove with armouring. Throwing down the gauntlet means offering a challenge.

Then we have gauntlet No. 2, as in running the gauntlet, which is entirely different. This comes from the Swedish word *gantlope*, meaning a passage between soldiers. There was an old military punishment where a solider had to run the gantlope — he ran through a passage of soldiers all armed with ropes to hit him. Thus we gain the modern meaning of run the gauntlet — to be attacked from all sides.

 Why does the word *gay* now seem to mean homosexual?

It's an example of evolution in a word's meaning. Gay still does mean happy, but it has developed a secondary meaning that has all but taken over from the first. The word comes to English from the Old French *gai*, meaning joy, mirth, light-hearted. But by the 11th century the word had developed a sub-meaning towards immoral, possibly even prostitution. In the mid-20th century another shade of meaning firmed up — homosexual; first of all it referred only to men, then to both sexes.

This latter meaning has become so firm that many poems and songs that included the word in its earlier sense have become unusable, e.g. the popular song from *The Maid of the Mountains*, 'A Bachelor Gay Am I'.

 Why do we express irritation by saying something *gets our goat*?

Dating from 1911, this is a very American expression but it matches up with a French expression, *prendre la chèvre*, to take the goat. There are three theories about this:

(1) Goats were a mainstay of European village life, and if someone stole a poor man's goat, then he became angry.

(2) A goat was often put into a stable as a companion for a horse. If the goat was stolen before a big race, the horse would become upset, and lose its competitive edge.

(3) Goat is short for goatee, as in beard, so if you got someone by the goatee, you would certainly annoy them.

 Q **What is the origin of *giddy goat*, as in 'Stop acting the giddy goat'?**

There are two possibilities. First, the image of a goat has, for many centuries, been associated with sin and even the devil, so it *might* be a way of hauling someone back onto the straight and narrow when they're misbehaving.

But goats do actually act quite skittishly sometimes and get a mad look in their eyes, so it might mean exactly what it says.

Is there any connection with the expression *horsing about*? I'm inclined to think that's straightforward too — a horse, left to its own devices, will often frisk and jump around. But, to a pragmatist, such behaviour is not at all constructive: the animal isn't hauling a cart or making money by winning a race. Hence horsing about probably means non-productive energy, and acting the giddy goat probably means lively and mischievous activity that could end up wrecking the garden.

 Q **Is the phrase *giving me gyp* anything to do with gypsies?**

No, it has nothing to do with gypsies. This is a lovely example of a verbal contraction, like goodbye (God be with you).

Originally, when something was irritating a person said, 'It's giving me gee-up', as in jerking a horse into action. Over the years the gee-up has simply shortened to gyp, but the meaning has stayed the same: a probably unpleasant sensation which has the effect of stimulating something.

84

Q **How did the expression *gobsmacked* originate?**

Gob is an ancient word for mouth in North-West Britain. The combination of gob with smacked, meaning absolutely astonished, is believed to have arisen in Liverpool and was used fairly commonly there. But it didn't leap into national or international use until 1991, as the direct result of one incident. A member of the British Labour Party made a particular comment about the government's health service, and when this remark was reported to the chairman of the Conservative Party, he said he was gobsmacked. This announcement made *huge* headlines, and overnight the word became common parlance first in Britain, and then everywhere. So although he didn't originate it, the honour of popularising the word goes directly to Chris Patten in 1991.

Other people have bestowed instant fame on common expressions that had existed beforehand: Sir Edmund Hillary — 'because it was there', Churchill — 'Iron Curtain', Marie Antoinette — 'Let them eat cake', Fred Dagg — 'Get in behind', Barry Crump — 'a good keen man', Princess Anne — 'Naff off'.

Q **God stiffen the crows — is this Shakespearean?**

No, it's English but much later than Shakespeare. The expression seems to have grown out of a 19th-century English oath, God stiffen it, meaning render it useless, destroy it, or sometimes said just as a violent expletive.

It particularly caught the fancy of Australians; there are three versions across the Tasman: God stiffen the crows, the lizards or the snakes. And it means much the same as it always did.

Later, towards the 20th century, Australians developed a slightly shorter and different version — stone the crows (possibly from 'stun'), which is closely related to the original.

Why do we describe someone as going on the ran-tan?

The word ran-tan itself is thought to be an echoic — imitating a sound from another source. What it was echoing was the noise made during a very old British custom.

Years ago, if a person was alleged to be a wife-beater, villagers would gather outside the house and beat pots and pans and kettles and buckets, making a terrible noise as they marched round and round the property — hence the word ran-tan, from the sound they made. This was repeated for three nights.

In time, the custom transferred to other misdemeanours; one recorded case concerned a woman who made unkind gossipy remarks about another woman, so the maligned woman's friends gathered and ran-tanned the house of the gossip, resulting in 23 arrests.

The last known ran-tan of this specific folk-custom kind occurred in 1930, but the word has remained, associated with a noisy progress to somewhere, and it has become strongly connected with jollity and drinking, rather than criticism and condemnation.

Did the old song 'The Mountains of Mourne' give rise to the expression gold-digger?

'The Mountains of Mourne' was composed by Percy French who died in 1920. But the expression a gold-digger, meaning a person who befriends the rich in hope of enjoying the fruits of their wealth, is believed to have originated in the United States around 1925. So although the song and the expression did arise about the same time, one speaks of digging gold literally, and the song mentions digging gold in imagination. And we have to remember that expressions about digging for gold aren't found only in that Irish song: it was a common description of people who actually did dig during gold rushes, even in New Zealand.

Q Where does the expression *a golden boy* come from?

In *Cymbeline* Shakespeare wrote that 'Golden lads and girls all must/As chimney sweepers come to dust.' The expression was possibly already known to him when he penned those words, and it's not too difficult to imagine the phrase golden lads slowly changing to golden boys or boy.

The phrase took on a more prominent position in 1920 when a striking statue was erected in Manitoba in Canada. It was of an athletic young man, gold covered, and was called The Golden Boy.

But the event that really nailed it into the public's mindscape was when the famous American playwright Clifford Odets's play *Golden Boy* was staged in 1937. The drama concerned a young Italian-American who was supposed to be a violinist but took up boxing, and then broke his hand. He realised he could never fulfil the family's ambition that he become a star fiddler, and determined to make the same success and fame as a boxer. Filmed in 1939 with William Holden, the play was then made into a stage musical in 1964, with the story changed to that of a young black man, starring Sammy Davis Jr. Most people who'd never heard the expression before certainly heard it after a famous play, movie and musical.

There are many expressions mentioning gold and golden: the ancient Greek legends about the golden ass and the golden fleece, and the golden apple of the judgement of Paris. There is the golden calf in the Bible, and the golden horde of Mongol Tartars.

In modern times we often hear of a golden handshake, an expression dating from 1964 meaning a considerable payment made to an employee whose service is prematurely terminated. This generated golden hello, which is bonus money promised to someone if they will leave one organisation and join another, and golden handcuffs, which is money paid to keep someone in their job when they've been made another offer.

Some of those expressions concern money but some of them don't really mean money at all: for instance, golden oldie doesn't mean a rich old person, and golden boy doesn't necessarily mean a rich boy. The expression is focused more on someone being special or much loved by family and friends; whether famous or not, he is as precious as gold would be.

 Where is or was *Gondwanaland* and where does the word come from?

German meteorologist and geophysicist Alfred Wegener believed all present continents derived from one large supercontinent comprising all the Earth's land mass. His belief was published early in the 20th century. He called his continent Pangea, and believed that when the mass broke up over 100 million years ago, it formed a northern supercontinent called Laurasia and a southern supercontinent called Gondwanaland. Those two continents subsequently broke to form the land masses we recognise on Earth today. The name Gondwanaland appears to come from a place in central India called Gondwana, where three million people called Gonds still live.

Q **What is the origin of *gone for a Burton*?**

There are several versions but two are related to Burton's beer and Burton's menswear. Eric Partridge says that, about 1939, the RAF would say someone had gone for a glass of Burton's ale when actually he was missing or dead after an air raid. The brewery's big advertising campaign of the time showed a huge crowd of people with one blank person-shaped hole in the middle — he'd gone for a Burton (ale), and that is thought to be the origin of the pilots' expression.

In Blackpool, the RAF wireless officers' training school was in a Burton's clothing store and those who failed their tests were said to have gone for a Burton.

Another possible explanation is that a bomb dump which exploded near Burton-on-Trent may have generated the phrase gone for a Burton. But really, nobody is sure.

Q **Where does the phrase *gone with the wind* originate?**

English poet Ernest Dowson, who died in 1900, was responsible for what has become a very famous phrase in our language. His poem *Non Sum Qualis Eram Bonae Sub Regno Cynarae*, published in 1896, included these lines:

I have forgot much Cynara! gone with the wind,
Flung roses, roses riotously with the throng,
Dancing, to put thy pale, lost lilies out of mine;
But I was desolate and sick of an old passion
Yea, all the time, because the dance was long:
I have been faithful to thee, Cynara! in my fashion.

Q **Why do people exclaim *Gordon Bennett* when things aren't going right?**

Gordon Bennett is a well known expression in times of shock or stress. There are a few scholars who believe that Gordon Bennett is a mangled way of saying God and St Bennett, but the over-whelming belief is that he was a real person, called James Gordon Bennett, born in the United States in 1841.

Gordon Bennett caused a major scandal in New York in 1877, when at a very grand party he got drunk and mistook the fireplace in the main lounge for a lavatory. Then he had to fight a duel because of what he'd done in the fireplace, after which he escaped to Europe.

In 1887 he established the Paris edition of the *New York Herald* (his father had founded the original paper), which eventually made money, and lived an extravagant life. He had an enormous yacht with its own Turkish bath and 24-hour masseur. There was also a padded cell to house a cow which provided fresh milk at sea. In restaurants, he would eat up large, then simply offer the proprietor a handful of banknotes saying, 'Take what you think is right.'

He liked mutton chops for lunch and because a certain restaurant in Monte Carlo served them, he went there frequently. One day there were other people sitting at the table he liked, and, in a pique, he told the owner he would buy the restaurant on the spot. He did and, after lunch, gave the restaurant to the waiter who'd served him — his name was Ciro and eventually Mr Ciro's three restaurants became among the best-known in the world.

Mr Bennett's impetuous and free spending continued throughout his life and he became very famous. A street in Paris is named after him — Avenue Gordon-Bennett.

By the time he died in 1918, people were saying his name as an expression of wonderment or extravagant disaster. They may have wanted to say 'Oh God', but in those days any blasphemous expression was socially unacceptable, and the name of Gordon Bennett sounded close enough to the real thing — plus it had the added frisson of actually being the name of someone synonymous with outrage and shock.

Q **Why is someone called *gormless*?**

It's a very old word in English, though it actually comes from the Norse language in Scandinavia, where in ancient times the word *gaumr* meant heed, paying close attention. Gaumr travelled into Old English and by the 18th century had become used only in the negative — *gaum*less, meaning not paying attention, being dull and stupid. The spelling changed about 1900 years ago into *gorm*less but it has always stayed negative. You seldom hear of anyone being gorm-ful.

People sometimes use gorm in the positive, e.g. 'He never gormed me' or 'We take no gorm of him', both demonstrating the exact meaning of gorm, which is heed.

Q **Why is a *grandfather clock* so called?**

Big tall clocks with pendulums are correctly called long case-clocks — always were and still are. But in 1876 a man called Henry Clay Work wrote a song about the fact that his grandfather owned a big tall clock. Within a very short time the song, 'My

Grandfather's Clock', went round the world, and its title experienced a mysterious shift. Quite quickly the apostrophe was dropped and instead of the clock belonging to the grandfather, the word grandfather was used to describe the clock itself — a grandfather clock.

The term is now fairly universal and has widened to include slightly smaller long-case clocks which are known as grandmother clocks.

 Why, in the same generation, do you have a *grandmother* and her sister, a *great-aunt*?

This is very mysterious. It would appear that for many centuries the prefix grand was most commonly used to describe the generation beyond one's parents — as in grandmother, grand-aunt, grand-uncle.

Grandmother and grandfather had all kinds of shortened versions — grandmama, granny, gran, grandma — and those are all changing: the d's are slowly being eliminated and you'll hear and see granpa and granma.

The prefix grand remains for one's parents' parents but in the late 19th century or somewhere in the 20th century the prefix grand was moved away from parents' aunts and uncles, who became great-aunts and great-uncles.

 ***Doesn't let grass grow under his feet* — how long has that expression been around?**

A very long time — it first appeared in print in the 1500s. Obviously the expression refers to an energetic person who does not allow things around him or her to drift or grow fallow.

It has turned up in English in various forms — it used to be no grass grows on his heel or no grass grows under his heel, which could perhaps be related to the rolling stone gathering no moss. Both of those expressions appeared in print in the 1500s. A century later the grass growing under the feet had settled down into the version we're familiar with today. You'll find it in an old book about the history of four-footed beasts, published in 1607, when it talks about hares: 'The hare leaps and lets no grass grow under his feet'.

 Why is the room where actors gather and rest backstage always called the *green room*?

Before the invention of efficient night lighting, theatres presented performances only in daylight. Candles could be used for smallish performances and then eventually illumination by gas lighting became common. In early New Zealand, the Aurora Theatre in Wellington used lighting provided by whale blubber.

Solo performers were highlighted on-stage by a rudimentary spotlight that burned lime (calcium hydroxide) to extreme heat and gave out a hard white light. Hence the expression in the limelight.

Both gas lighting and limelight are very glaring when you have to look into them for a long period, so the custom arose that the resting room backstage be painted a cooling restful green. (There is a theory that the colour green is placid, and also that green is the colour the human eye needs least of, in order to see efficiently.)

For many years the green room was actually green; the term has appeared in print since 1834. Theatres and television studios still have waiting rooms called green rooms. Modern lighting is not as harsh, so the rooms no longer need to be painted green, but the name remains.

Why is an expert or skilled person called a *gun*?

Within the culture of the American gangland, people were assigned various roles: the banker looked after the money, the car man organised getaways and the gunman had the job of resolving a situation, if necessary, by shooting. Gunman eventually became shortened to just gun, and that word became shorthand for an effective person who didn't muck around but got things done. Now it seems to mean the best.

It was probably introduced to New Zealand during the Second World War when hundreds of American troops came here, bringing their own slang culture with them.

 Where does *I'll have your guts for garters* come from?

The meaning is fairly clear: to put it politely, you have reached a fair level of annoyance with someone, and you propose to wrench out their innards and use them tied around your legs to keep your socks up.

But the expression isn't polite at all and never has been. It's been used in English since the 16th century. We know that it's never been polite, because the first time it appeared in print was in a rather grand play called *The Scottish History of James IV* written by Robert Greene who, according to contemporary critics, was a man who knew a lot about low life.

So it wasn't exactly a surprise to the critics when, in that play, one of the nobles at the court of King James said to another 'I'll make garters of thy guts' and that was first heard late in the 1500s. Slightly modified, the expression has stayed in the language ever since.

It did go into obscurity for some time, and was known during the 19th and early 20th century as being peculiar to the slang of racecourses. But then it surfaced into what might be called common parlance and although curiously, with the invention of stretch-knit fabrics, garters have become almost obsolete, you still hear people say, 'I'll have your guts for garters'.

Q

What is the explanation for *ha-ha*, as in 'The mansion had a ha-ha'?

A *ha-ha* is a deep ditch that is dug around the perimeters of a stately home to allow uninterrupted views of the surrounding landscape and prevent livestock from straying into the grounds. There's one at Glyndebourne that stops the cows in the next field from walking among the picnicking opera patrons.

The origin of the name isn't very exciting. It is quite old, probably 18th-century, and it is thought simply to be the exclamation of surprise people made if they inadvertently fell into a ha-ha.

Q

What is the origin of the phrase *hail-fellow-well-met*?

Hale comes from the Old Norse word *heill* meaning complete and all in working order — thus healthy and strong. It survives in the modern English word *whole*. The word hale or hail became an exclamation of welcome, hoping that the person you meet up with is in good health — there's an echo of it in modern hi. It also survives as part of the word wassail, which really is two Old Norse words, *ves heill*, which became the Old English *wes hal*, meaning be healthy. It is used as an exclamation before having a drink of liquor, especially amid friends and with a feeling of good fellowship.

So hail-fellow-well-met literally means 'I'm pleased to see you and I hope you're in good health' though today's dictionaries give such synonyms as genial in an over-familiar, rather ingratiating way.

Why do we say a person is *happy as a sandboy*?

This has nothing to do with beaches and summer. It originates from English pubs and houses which, in earlier centuries, often had slabs of stone for flooring in the kitchen and living areas. It was quite common practice to scrub a stone floor thoroughly and then sprinkle clean sand over it. The sand, and anything that spilled on it, could be swept out each day. But the sand didn't come from beaches — it came from ground-down blocks of sandstone, and was delivered to houses in bags carried by donkeys driven by young lads.

The housewives in early days had a fairly grim time. Every day they swept the dirty sand off the floor, scrubbed the stones and waited for the sandboy to bring a new bag. The traditional belief is that these women envied the sand-delivery lads their apparently free and cheerful life, in comparison with their existence, scrubbing the same floor every day. Hence the expression grew — happy as a sandboy.

The stone floors and the delivering of sand are now long gone but the expression has remained, and it might be that, over the years, this old phrase has come to fit an entirely new context: sunshine, sandcastles and swimsuits.

 Why do we say someone is *happy as Larry*? Who was Larry?

This is another question that doesn't have a clear and definitive answer. We do know what the expression means — it means very happy indeed — and we know that it seems to have originated in Australia about 100 years ago.

But it is not clear who Larry was, or if he existed. There was a well-known boxer in 19th-century Australia called Larry Foley, and there is one school of thought that the expression came about because he was relentlessly cheerful, in spite of his profession.

But another school of thought says that Larry is an abbreviated form of larrikin. As a word, larrikin is not strictly Australian; it originates in one of the dialects of England, but you're unlikely to hear the word used in Britain nowadays. Somehow it took on in Australia and bypassed its homeland. In modern Australia a larrikin is a happy-go-lucky young man.

So possibly Larry is happy because he's a natural larrikin, or possibly the expression is a legacy left to us from an otherwise forgotten boxer.

 Who wrote *'Happy Birthday'*?

The song was written by two sisters in Kentucky, Patty Hill and Mildred Smith. They intended it to be a song for starting the day in the schoolroom, and it was called 'Good Morning to All'. That was copyrighted, including the tune, in 1893.

But in 1924 a pirate publisher printed it without permission, and altered the words, without permission, from 'Good Morning' to 'Happy Birthday'. This was a huge success and the song was sung all over the place and republished several times, until one of the Hill sisters got sick of it, and sued.

She won the case, and the court declared in 1935 that the tune of 'Happy Birthday' was owned by the Hill sisters, and every time it is used commercially, a royalty payment must be made to the Hill family.

 Hash is the common name for the # sign on the bottom row of your phone buttons but the same kind of design in artwork is always called hatch. Why are there two words for the same thing?

When artists fill in an area by drawing vertical lines and then put horizontal lines over them, the resultant little squares are called hatching, or cross-hatch. But the little noughts and crosses sign on your phone, which is essentially that same thing, is customarily called the hash key.

The only explanation I can offer is that they aren't two words at all but the same word, just said differently. They are both derived from the French word *hacher*, meaning to chop up, and in their English version, they both mean that.

Hatch is to make cross lines and finish up with a lot of squares — the space is broken up. And hash is to cut into pieces, as in hash brown potatoes, or making a hash of something, meaning you have broken something from the form it should have been in.

These different pronunciations existed before that sign ever went on phone dials, so I simply can't explain why we call the phone sign hash instead of hatch.

Q **Do we say that chickens *hatch* out of eggs because they break up the eggshell when they do so?**

No, it's an entirely different word. English has borrowed three separate words with three separate meanings, but unfortunately they've all finished up being pronounced much the same.

Cross-hatch, as in drawing noughts and crosses, and hash, both come from the French *hacher*, to break up. Then there's hatch meaning a sort of opening, like a serving hatch, or down the hatch, from an old German and Dutch word *hec*, meaning gate. Then there's chickens hatching and yes, they do break up the shell but they're not doing it in French. That hatch comes from an old German word *hecken*, which is to do with birds mating and breeding and, as a result of their mating, we speak of the chickens hatching, or a hatch of chickens — the new breed.

It's also that word we use when speaking of people hatching a plot because they plot closely together — like birds mating.

Q **Where does the cricketing term *hat trick* come from?**

It was an old custom of cricket players that if a bowler successively bowled out three opponents, then he was entitled to buy a new hat at the club's expense. The expression has come to mean anything successful which is repeated three times.

Q What is the origin of the expression the *head sherang*?

Sherang, the boss, is from an Urdu word *serang*, meaning the principal authority, especially of a ship, a commander. The word has somehow floated into English use as meaning the absolute boss, for instance the chief executive officer or the managing director.

It can be pronounced serang but New Zealanders usually say sherang, and add the word head, which makes a tautology, like saying 'rich millionaire'.

Q Why are young cows called *heifers*?

Young cows are called heifers because in this language that's been the word for a young cow for over 800 years. The Old English *heahfore* has hardly changed, and has been used in New Zealand since 1839.

Q Why do Americans drop the 'h' at the beginning of the word *herbs*?

The English language has thousands of words borrowed from other languages and a great many of these are French. French people do not pronounce the letter h at the beginning of a word, and it has been a linguistic custom in English for many centuries to copy this pronunciation, as in honour or heirloom — and you will still hear meticulously correct people say an 'otel.

Herbs is an odd one. It was borrowed into English from French (originally from Latin) and normally, people speaking English have not followed the rule about dropping the initial h. But curiously, Americans have followed the old rule and customarily drop the h at the beginning of herbs, as if it were still a French word. To add one inconsistency to another, if a man is called Herb, Americans do pronounce the h at the beginning.

How do you tell the difference between *herbs* and *spices*?

Tricky — a bit like deciding whether a tomato is a vegetable or a fruit. (Tomato is actually a fruit because it has seeds. And sake is not a wine: it is made from grain so is properly a beer.)

In this case, herbs are everything green and all the rest are spices (seeds, stalks, bark, dried leaves, stamens).

 What is the origin of the odd-sounding expression *Hey baba rhubarb*?

This is a product of the jazz era, when the word bop was invented to describe a new kind of music that was fast and rhythmic with complex harmony and slang lyrics. Bop engendered several variations, such as re-bop, meaning, I suppose, do the bop again, and then someone put 'Hey' at the beginning, as a sort of attention-getting exclamation.

Thus, the phrase originally was sung as hey, bop a-re-bop which somehow, through usage and bastardisation, ended up as hey baba rhubarb, which is even more meaningless than the original.

 We often hear of people having *high jinks*. What on earth are jinks, high or otherwise?

The word jinks, meaning games, has been used for about 200 years. Nobody is clear how the word came into being, but it's most often heard in the phrase high jinks which is, or was, a definite game.

Sir Walter Scott used the term in his novel *Guy Mannering*, set in the time of George III. The characters play the game high jinks by throwing dice, and whoever is *it*, has to, for a certain period of time, act as a fictitious character, someone quite different from themselves. Among people of the time, this was considered terribly funny, and the phrase has come to mean lively good times.

Q We talk about *Hobson's choice* — was there ever a real Hobson?

Yes indeed, he was a real person, in 16th- and 17th-century Britain. Thomas Hobson operated a carrying and horse-hiring business in Cambridge, and he had plenty of horses. But Mr Hobson was very careful about the well-being of his animals, and very strict about letting each one out only in the order of their having rested. He always kept the ones who'd been properly rested near the door.

So when you went to his stables, no matter how many horses it seemed there were to choose from, you had to hire the one nearest the door. You really had no choice at all, and that's what the saying means. Mr Hobson died in 1631 and the saying has been around ever since.

Q Why are young New Zealand sheep called *hoggets*?

It is an English word, derived from old Celtic. In Britain it was used to mean a young sheep, not yet shorn.

The use of the word varies enormously, sometimes even from district to district. It is occasionally heard in Britain to mean young pigs, and even more occasionally a year-old colt. And to confuse the issue further, the word hogget can very *very* occasionally be found referring to a young goat.

Amidst all that, in New Zealand the word hogget has moved firmly onto sheep since 1860 and has stayed there.

There is still a certain amount of variation. If you ask three New Zealand farmers from three different districts exactly what a hogget is, you might get three slightly different answers. But, in general, a very young sheep is called a lamb until it's approximately one year old when it loses its two centre-front milk teeth and grows adult teeth. It then stops being a lamb and for the next 12 months it is called a hogget or a two-tooth. Both terms are very common and mean the same — hogget and two-tooth.

But although the beasts themselves can freely be referred to as either hoggets or two-tooths, the latter term is never used to describe the meat. You can find a butcher selling hogget-meat, but you won't find one selling two-tooth meat, although they are exactly the same thing.

The youngest variety of sheep-meat sold is lamb, which is up to approximately one year old. That is followed by hogget and from then on, mutton.

Q What is the origin of *holus-bolus*?

Holus-bolus usually means the total, the whole lot, and it's thought to be derived from an original Greek phrase *holos bolos* which means all at once, the entire lump. And English people gradually rounded that Greek phrase into holus bolus, which has a slightly jocular air to it.

Q Where does the phrase *home sweet home* come from?

It was the title of a song that was the big hit of a London musical written in 1823 by Sir Henry Rowley Bishop. The opera, which was called *Clari*, hasn't lasted but the song is still a favourite and the phrase is often used without the music.

Q How did the word *honeymoon* come about?

There are two possible answers to this one.

Honey has always meant sweetness. Then there was the cynical old feeling that the initial thrill in a marriage would last only until the phase of the moon repeated itself a month. The two ideas joined: the period after a marriage would be as sweet as honey, but only for the length of one moon.

The concept has been around at least since the 17th century. Here's a piece published in 1656: 'Those married persons that love well at first and decline in affection afterwards — it is honey now, but it will change with the moon.'

In Gilbert and Sullivan's *The Mikado*, when the person being married is going to be executed one month later he is told 'You'll live at least a honeymoon', meaning one month.

The custom also developed that people who could afford it went for a holiday after their wedding, which was known as a honeymoon trip. This became so common that the word trip was eventually dropped and honeymoon meant just the holiday after the wedding.

The old concept still survives, however, and can also be used, say, about a business going into a decline, or a political party. You hear people say that the honeymoon is over: the moon has changed and the sweetness has run out!

There is another version of how the word came about. One scholarly source claims that the term honeymoon has risen over the years from an old Scandinavian custom of drinking fermented honeyed wines immediately after marriage, because they were believed to be aphrodisiac.

Q **Is *hooey*, as in 'a lot of hooey', a Maori expression?**

No, it's not Maori; *hooey* actually comes from Ireland. Once upon a time in Ireland the village of Ballyhooly in County Cork became famous for its noisy street debates, and its name is thought to be the origin of the expression ballyhoo, meaning a lot of noise. The expression was in use by comedians in British music halls in the 1880s. With the growth of advertising and media, ballyhoo extended its meaning to describe what we nowadays call spin doctoring or hype— defined by Brewer as 'misleading, inflated or highly exaggerated advertising publicity'.

Round about 1920 the word hooey became common in the United States. Its origin isn't exactly clear but it's possible that this is a shortened version of ballyhoo which itself is a shortened version of Ballyhooly. And by then it meant just something nonsensical. There is also a school of thought that hooey is a variation on an-other nonsense word phooey, which derives ultimately from Yiddish.

Interestingly, there's no direct connection between all those words — Ballyhooly, ballyhoo, hooey and phooey — and the similar words hooligan and hooley. Those last two are thought to derive from a semi-fictitious Irish family called Houlihan who lived in London and lived somewhat riotously. From their name came the word hooligan, an unruly noisy fellow, and then hooley, an unruly noisy party. Semantically, the words are not related: the only connection is that they all imply that Irishmen are noisy.

The Maori word hui, meaning a meeting, a seminar, a convention, has the same sound (a homophone) but no connection at all with hooey, meaning nonsense.

Q Where does the word *hoon* come from?

The word's actual origin is unknown but it has gone through distinct changes of meaning. Before the Second World War a hoon was a loutish exhibitionist, much as he is today (it always seems to be male). But during the war the same word underwent a complete reversal of meaning. People who were conscientious objectors on other than religious grounds were known to the military as hoons (the others were called religoes). They would have been thoughtful people, firm in their philosophical conviction that war was wrong.

The word remained in use, but reverted to its earlier sense. A few grammatical extensions also exist: hoonish, hoonism, hooning, hoondom, hoon around, hoon it up, a bit of a hoon, hoon-chaser (traffic police) and hoon-bin (place where drunken football louts are put to cool off).

An Auckland wind instrument music group, available for freelance gigs, even called themselves The Newton Hoons, presumably a nice wordplay on the fact that they played horns.

Q Why is part of Christchurch called *Hoon Hay*?

Some people still think it has a Chinese derivation, but diligent research by Mr R.R. Beauchamp, a long-time resident of

Hoon Hay, showed that, in 1852, a Captain Wickham emigrated from England to this part of Christchurch, having come from a farm in Derbyshire called Hoon Hay.

In the ancient dialect of Derbyshire, *hoon* means a hill or even a slight mound, and *hay* means an enclosure; it is the ancestor of our modern word hedge. So, the Wickham family's farm in England was on a hill and surrounded by a hedge, and their property in Christchurch inherited the name, which was eventually applied to the whole suburb.

What has a horse to do with a radish, as in *horseradish*?

The *Stobart Cook's Encyclopaedia* explains that the word horse, when applied to any foodstuff, indicates that the product is big, strong or coarse.

For example, there's horse mackerel (which is an inferior type of fish), horse mushrooms (which are large and tough), presumably horse chestnuts as well, and also horseradish which, compared with ordinary salad radishes, is large, tough and more pungent.

What is the origin of the old custom of hanging a *horseshoe* over a mantelpiece or doorway or giving one to a bride to bring luck?

New Zealand academic Professor Paul Dunmore has associated the symbolism of horseshoes with animist superstition, animism being the belief that natural objects and phenomena possess souls. Several ingredients combine in this belief about horseshoes, and some of them go back a long, long way.

Ingredient No. 1: horses. For many centuries horses have carried an image of strength and nobility; as far back as the Ice Age they were depicted in cave art, even before they became tamed and domesticated. So for a very long time the horse has been perceived as a good thing.

Ingredient No. 2: iron. There was an ancient belief that iron warded off evil. Ancient houses often had heavy iron nails studded into the doors, because these helped to divert bad luck and disease.

Ingredient No. 3: witches. Belief in witches goes way, way back, and one of the things thought about witches was that they were scared of horses. Witches travelled on broomsticks because they wouldn't ride on horses, and any symbol related to horses was enough to frighten a witch away from your house.

Ingredient No. 4: the shape. We're getting closer now. A horseshoe is roughly the shape of a crescent moon, which for centuries has been regarded as a symbol of positive things like fertility, good fortune and hope. It still is — in non-Christian countries the Red Cross is called the Red Crescent and has the new moon shape as its symbol.

So, bit by bit, we're getting the picture that the horseshoe had some affiliated powers because it was associated with horses, it was made of the powerful substance iron and, by coincidence, it was in the magic shape of a crescent moon.

The ancient Greeks were regarding horseshoes with respect in the 4th century, and the symbol was adopted by ancient Rome as well. The horseshoe was firmly established in people's minds as a symbol of good things, and this belief was passed on to the newly emerging Christian religion. In the English-speaking culture, two further ingredients made the horseshoe's reputation even more solid.

Ingredient No. 5: Dunstan. Ten centuries ago in Britain, a legend grew around a man called Dunstan, who was working as a blacksmith. One day an odd-looking creature came to his forge and asked for shoes to be put on his hooves. Recognising that the hooves were cloven, Dunstan realised this was the Devil himself, so told him that to do the job properly he had to tie him to the wall; the customer agreed. Dunstan then shod the hooves, but deliberately made such a painful job of it that the Devil was shrieking with pain and begging to be released. Dunstan then told the Devil he would release him from the ropes only if he promised never again to enter a house with a horseshoe above the door; once again, the Devil agreed.

Dunstan eventually became Archbishop of Canterbury and a saint, and although the blacksmith story is somewhat fanciful, it did a great deal to encourage the belief that a horseshoe was not a bad thing to have around.

Ingredient No. 6: Lord Nelson. This was quite an influential matter, which occurred much later, in 1805. Lord Horatio Nelson was a firm believer in the power of horseshoes, and everyone knew that a genuine horseshoe was nailed to the mast of his ship *Victory* when Britain triumphed at the Battle of Trafalgar, thus ending Napoleon's hopes of invading England.

So these various ingredients have combined into a centuries-old belief that horseshoes are good. And, remember, to be effective, the horseshoe must have its ends pointing upwards; otherwise its good qualities will simply drip out.

Is the horseshoe given to a bride anything to do with attaching old shoes to the bridal car after a wedding? No, they are two entirely separate customs. But they both carry similar images of what we nowadays would call good vibes, and fertility.

Q Is or was the term *hotbed* actually agricultural?

A hotbed is a glass-covered bed of soil, usually heated by fermenting material, used for propagating plants or forcing early vegetables. The word has widened to mean a situation offering ideal conditions for the growth of an idea or activity, especially one considered bad.

Q Why do we say that we *hull* strawberries?

Hull comes from the Old High German *helawa*, meaning to hide, and filtered into Old English first as *helan* and then *hulu*, taking on the meaning of the outer casing of something. The main body of a ship is the hull — you can't see what's going on inside — and the same name is sometimes given to the outer casing of a rocket or missile.

The calyx that protects and hides the bud of a strawberry flower remains in position after the flower has opened, and long after the fruit has outgrown it. But this persistent little calyx, although it's no longer hiding anything, is still called the hull.

So there developed this verb, to hull, which means to remove the outside. To hull a ship means to pierce the outer covering, and to hull strawberries means to remove the little calyx or hull that used to hide the flower.

Q **Where does the word *humbug* come from?**

This very old word, meaning trickery and deceit, has been in use for over 200 years. Its exact origin is not certain, but it's possible that it grew out of the old expression hum and haw, meaning uncertainty or delay, plus bug.

Nowadays there are two added factors. Humbug has developed a connotation of useless pretension — 'what a lot of humbug' — about some unnecessary paperwork or bureaucracy. And in Britain the word is used to describe a type of hard, striped, boiled sweet, although there seems to be no clear connection between that and the other meaning of fraud and imposture.

Q **What is the origin of *humdinger*?**

It's believed this word originated in the armed services, initially in the United States, and then moved to Britain about 1940.

It means spectacularly effective, and since it was originally applied to crafts of war, the derivation is thought to come from combining the two words hum, meaning the hum of speed, with dinger, a slang word for something good. Together they make humdinger — a humming, speedy motor which does a dinger of a good job.

Why, when things are boring, do we say they're *humdrum*?

This is a very old word, dating from the mid-16th century. The only explanation of its origin is that it's another of those words which has a repetitive bit added to amplify the effect: hum, meaning a steady, even sound without variety, has the echo word drum joined on to double the suggestion of boredom.

Q **What is the origin of the expression** *hurly-burly*?

Hurly-burly, meaning uproar and confusion, has been in use since the 1600s, and in those days *hurling* meant making a lot of noise. People added a rhyming word to give the expression emphasis — so hurly meant noisy, but hurly-burly meant very noisy.

Thus, in *that* context, the word burly doesn't mean anything — it's just a repetitive sound that adds to the first word.

Q **Where does the word** *hurray* **come from?**

It is a variation on hurrah. There was fanciful belief that this was a Slavonic word *hu-raj*, meaning paradise, but scholars now discount that and believe that hurrah is a variant on huzza, believed to be a 17th-century sailors' cheer, possibly from German *hurra*, which means much the same thing.

In New Zealand the word, spelt hooray, has developed a parallel but totally different meaning: as a form of goodbye. It has absolutely no connection with the Maori phrase haere ra.

 Shakespeare sometimes says *huswif* **— does this mean housewife or hussy?**

Both — in Shakespeare's time the word huswif could mean either.

Housewife has gone through numerous spellings over the centuries: huswife, husewif, huswyf, hyswif, huzzif. Generally these were all pronounced as 'hussif'.

Two different parallel meanings and two separate spellings evolved: (1) housewife, a woman, presumably respectable, who managed a household, and (2) hussy (a contraction of housewife), a woman of bold mien and probably loose morals.

The word and its two meanings were in a transitory phase during Shakespeare's time and he appears to use it in both senses, for instance in *Othello*, written about 1604. To avoid confusion, modern editors sometimes change whichever word Shakespeare originally used into either housewife or hussy, depending on the context in which it appears.

One slightly different survivor of the old word is a little folding sewing kit much used by the military, which is still called a hussif or housewife.

But in simple terms, the modern words housewife and hussy, though now totally different in meaning, stem from the same source. (Similarly, Miss, Mrs and Ms all developed from one original word, mistress, but have evolved into three separate terms with slightly different meanings.)

Q What does the phrase *I should cocoa* mean?

It comes from Cockney rhyming slang. The phrase when used in full is 'I should coffee and cocoa', meaning 'I should say so' — I agree or I affirm what you're saying.

Q Is the word *icon* being used nowadays in its proper sense? Can a living person correctly be called an icon?

The word icon comes from the Greek *eikon*, meaning image, and was originally used in English to describe a representation of Jesus or his mother, or a saint, painted in oil in the Byzantine style, and on a wooden panel. So the word has a connotation of veneration and worship, but that isn't necessary because in its strictly original sense it can just mean an image, a representation or even a symbol.

Since the early 1900s the word has been used quite widely to refer to famous people, especially those who are regarded as cult figures. It was often said of the Princess of Wales. In New Zealand, Sean Fitzpatrick and Colin Meads are rugby icons and Sir Edmund Hillary is an icon of mountaineering. But keeping the word's real meaning in mind, it accurately should be used only to describe someone who actually represents an ideal, demonstrates supremacy, is the focal point of something admired. If the word is used too much, it will lose its power.

And the oldest meaning of all has the newest usage. The little picture on a computer screen that guides you towards a particular action is often not a true representation of what is going to happen, but just a symbol, and that too is, quite rightly, called an icon.

There's no clear rule about an icon being dead. It might be possible to complain that the word's meaning has been debased because people referred to as icons are very seldom sacred, but it seems there's no need for them to be dead.

Q **Is the word *illegitimate* still acceptable?**

In 1840 New Zealand inherited the law of England, which clearly defined legitimacy and illegitimacy. In 1894 New Zealand modified the situation slightly with the passing of the Legitimation Act, which was modified again in 1921 and 1939, but the concept of legitimacy and illegitimacy remained and so did the wording.

Then in 1968 Ralph Hanan, the Minister of Justice, introduced to Parliament the Status of Children bill. Among comments on the proposal were Sir Leslie Munro's declaration that the morality behind the bill was that 'illegitimacy was not the fault of the child'. After formal parliamentary processes that bill became law in January 1970. The act uses the phrase 'born out of wedlock' instead of the word illegitimate, so the word was declared unacceptable within the context of an Act of Legislation.

But that's the only place. Interestingly enough, discussions in Parliament concerning the bill used the word illegitimate quite freely — as well as Sir Leslie Munro's comment already mentioned, Matiu Rata stated at one point that 'the disquieting problem of illegitimacy remained'.

So, as I understand it, the current status of the word is that it has been removed from legislation because of social implications to the child, but the word still means exactly the same as it always did, and there is no legal ban on using it in any other context.

 Why are instructions on printed music always written in the *Italian* language?

It's a matter of evolved custom. Some forms of classical music — symphonic and concerto music and opera — had crucial phases of their development in Italy, though it cannot be said that the Italians were *solely* responsible for their final traditions. German and Austrian and French composers were also heavily involved in the growth of what we call classical music. But the terms the Italian composers used became very widespread and dominant to the point that they're now almost universal.

I say almost universal because you will sometimes see music with German or French instructions on it, but I think it's fair to say that we're all comfortable with the Italian expressions, and it certainly makes things move more smoothly for international artists performing in different countries. Whatever they can't understand, they can all understand the conductor when he says *forte* or *piano* or *allegro*.

A similar thing happened with ballet, where the terms used are normally French. In Dunedin and Invercargill, ballerina Rowena Jackson learned all her ballet terms in French.

Perhaps the same thing is happening with computers, where the standard language appears to be English.

Q 'This is the house that Jack built' — does anyone know who *Jack* was?

The short answer is no, nobody is absolutely sure who Jack was. The poem is very old indeed; it is thought to have been in common use since the 13th century. One of the only clues to its age is the mention of the priest being shaven and shorn.

Officially 'The House that Jack Built' is described as poetry, which is based on the principle of accumulation, because it builds up and up and everything is connected to something else. For this reason, some scholars think it is based on an ancient Hebrew chant about a kid that a father bought for two coins, then along came a cat and ate the kid, then along came a dog and bit the cat . . . and so on.

Nursery rhymes are often political. 'The House that Jack Built' first appeared in print in 1750, and there is a theory that Jack in the poem is actually meant to be the mythical character John Bull, the symbolic representation of an Englishman, and that the rat is William the Conqueror. The symbol of John Bull has been around for several hundred years, so it's possible that Jack is John Bull, but we don't really know.

 Q 'Before you could say *Jack Robinson*' — was this Mr Robinson a real person?

Fanny Burney's novel *Evelina* used the expression in 1778 and in 1780 there was a British Secretary of the Treasury called John Robinson who is said to have had the expression uttered in Parliament in front of him, as a kind of joke, so the phrase was well established by the 18th century.

One scholar believes it stems from a very old play where a comedy character called Jack Robinson used to visit people and would rush out as soon as he arrived. But there is no evidence that Jack Robinson was a real person.

 What is the origin of *jalopy*, meaning a battered old car?

The word's origins are unknown. It was used in the 1930s and was perhaps an old brand of car. The spelling used to be jaloppi.

 Why do we say *Joe Bloggs*?

There is no specific point of origin here. The expression is known to have originated in Britain and simply means an ordinary bloke, aka Joe Public. In Australia and the United States he is called Joe Blow, or sometimes Joe Six-pack. In New Zealand he is sometimes Fred Bloggs.

 Who was *John Thomas*?

The expression John Thomas, a British euphemism for the male member, seems to have been used first in the 19th century. Originally the expression appears to have meant just a common ordinary man, and was sometimes interchangeable with John Willie, which meant the same thing. Both expressions appear to have undergone, shall we say, a narrowing down of focus.

John Thomas received its greatest exposure, as it were, in D.H. Lawrence's *Lady Chatterley's Lover*, which was published in a limited edition in 1928 but completely banned in the United States until 1959 and in Britain until 1960. Since then John Thomas has been . . . the full monty.

Why are Australian men often referred to as *jokers*?

In ordinary daily speech the word jokers refers to ordinary men and is often applied to local men who are completely devoid of wit or humour and so, strictly speaking, are not 'jokers' at all.

Joker, by dictionary definition, means a jolly fellow, but for many many years it was also used in Britain to mean an ordinary sort of bloke. Samuel Pepys used it exactly that way in 1669, writing that he had lunch with some old jokers — chaps, maybe somewhat lively over their food and drink, but certainly not distinguished gentlemen.

In the 19th century that use of the word somehow became stranded in Australia and New Zealand and is used in those countries far more than in other places, with the exact same connotation — ordinary fellows.

The word joker is very versatile and doesn't always mean a *pleasant* ordinary fellow. Its colour can change: a good joker, a bad joker, a mean joker, a wily joker . . . And sometimes it's anthropomorphised so you'll occasionally hear something like 'the puppy was a friendly little joker'.

 What does the word *jubilee* really mean?

The word jubilee actually means 50 years, if you abide by the meaning given in the Bible, so if you say 50th jubilee you're performing a tautology (saying the same thing twice) and if you say 75th jubilee you're performing an oxymoron (two statements of opposite meaning juxtaposed).

The word jubilee is Hebrew, *yobhel*, referring to the ancient practice of liberating slaves, restoring stolen property and planting certain crops, each seven-times-seven-years-plus-one, i.e. 50. But not everyone abides by what the Bible says, and words do tend to change their meanings over a period of several thousand years, and are influenced by other similar words, and jubilee has become modified for all those reasons.

Part of the modification came from the more recent Christian church, which gradually watered down the original 50 years to 25, and established various 25-year rituals that were called jubilees. At the time this was happening, the Latin word *jubilare*, meaning shouting out loud, became amalgamated with the old Hebrew word *yobhel* and we finished up, in English, with jubilee, which developed the double meaning of being a landmark number of years, *plus* a lot of noise and celebrating. Modern jubilees generally aren't quiet.

Growing out from the Christian modification there have been other uses of the word jubilee with other numbers of years — from very respectable sources. Queen Victoria held a 60th jubilee and Queen Elizabeth was the centre of a 25th jubilee.

This word has undergone a slight change of meaning, and is now freely used to mark any number of years past 19 which could be an excuse for a celebration. At least the title of one New Zealand movie won't bother pedantic people, because it's just called *Jubilee*.

K

Should it be spelt with a C or a K? It's spelt both ways but there's a preference for C because the word karking with a K is sometimes used in the United States, meaning what we call go-carts.

The word *cark* has been known in the North of England and Scotland for quite some decades, meaning to fret, worry and complain and cause anxiety. Charles Dickens, in *The Old Curiosity Shop*, uses carking of a character who is severely worried until 'all but dead'.

There are several other influences. Of course carcass means dead body, so that's a probable and strong contender for the origin of an abbreviation — cark. He's carked it, meaning to die, is sometimes thought to be of Australian origin, but in that country it's believed to date back to imitating the sound a crow makes because of an association between crows and carrion: death.

All these influences seem to have come together in Australia and New Zealand in the 20th century, because the expression to cark it has been freely used in these countries since the 1970s.

So although there is no absolutely clear answer to the origin of carking it, it is my opinion that several threads of language — the word carcass, the tradition of making crow noises when referring to death and the old Northern word for fretting and worrying — have blended together into the slang expression to kark, meaning to die. (Theatre folk, if they laugh on stage when they're not supposed to, say they're *corpsing*.)

Q Kaylied means drunk, but why?

There are various pronunciations — ky-leed, kay-lyd, kay-leed — and it seems to be very much a North England word. It's not uncommon — Vera Duckworth said it about Jack Duckworth on *Coronation Street*.

The origin is a bit confused. The word is believed to derive from the name of a plant called kali or saltwort, and that name is related to the Arabic word *alkili*. Saltwort was used in chemical manufacture to make potash. Somehow the name of the plant, kali, became used by children to describe a sherbert soft drink, and the word sherbert is used in a jokey way in North England to mean alcohol. So, kali and sherbert became interchangeable, and being drunk could be described as having had too much sherbert, which turned into a verb, kaylied, meaning drunk.

It's very common to use other terms instead of saying drunk: shickered, blotto, fried, oiled, full as a bull, squiffy, lathered, lit up, tight, tired and emotional, pie-eyed, plastered, primed, sozzled, tanked, stewed, out of his tree, off his face. And for the alcohol itself there are suds, sauce, amber liquid, strong drink.

Q What is the origin of the word *kerfuffle*?

It's very old Scottish Gaelic, two words that have been joined together: *car* means to twist and turn, and *fuffle* means to disarrange.

Q What does *putting the kibosh on something* mean?

It means to finish something, render it incapable of further action, to forbid a plan proceeding.

This is an old slang expression, probably around in spoken English for quite a while before Charles Dickens used it in print in the 19th century. It comes from the French, where *caboche* means to cut off the head. The term was used since ancient times in hunting to say that a deer had been killed and its head cut off. It came to be used by heralds — the people who design coats of arms — to describe pictures that show just the stag's head. This was a deer-head caboshed.

People in the streets picked up the expression from old English pubs, which usually have a painted sign outside. These inn signs were often painted by the same men who painted the local lord's coat of arms outside his mansion. Thus they knew the term caboshed, and if an inn had just a stag as its name, with a picture of a deer's head, people came to know that the painter would have called this a cabosh. Gradually it turned into kibosh or kybosh — to be given the chop.

Q **What is the origin of the term _kick the bucket_?**

There are at least four versions of why we use this very common expression.

(1) Bucket might have derived from the old French word _buquet_, meaning balance, and the word was sometimes used to describe the beam on which a pig was hung by its heels when it was being slaughtered. Presumably, in its death throes, the pig kicked against the _buquet_. Some farmers also said that the act of hauling the pig into the slaughter position was like pulling up a heavy bucket from a well, and the beam to which the pig was tied was referred to as a bucket, with the pig's feet hard up against it.

(2) A person arranging to hang himself could stand on a bucket while getting the rope in place, then kick the bucket away.

(3) There is an old European custom that workmates put out a bucket to collect donations for the widow of a man who'd died. Some people threw in money, but others who didn't like the deceased kicked the bucket as they went past.

(4) In ancient Egypt the bucket had a significance far beyond that which we give it. Egyptians regarded an empty bucket as a symbol of death, a body without life. When a person

did die, the ancient Egyptians said he or she had *khekh*ed the bucket, the word *khekh* meaning not kicked, but returned. The person was now dead, the bucket was empty.

 What is the origin of the expression *knickers in a twist* (or a *knot*)?

Knickers is a shortened form of the word Knickerbocker, which was the name of a fictitious Dutch family, invented by American writer Washington Irving. Because people in the United States thought that Dutchmen always wore long baggy trousers fastened below the knee or at the ankle, the word knickerbocker became the accepted word to describe trousers like that and you still occasionally hear it. Then the word knickerbocker became shortened over time to become just knickers, which were female underpants, especially those of a generous cut, like the original knickerbockers.

The saying don't get your knickers in a twist dates from the middle of the 19th century and is believed to have a feminine origin, as it evolved from don't get your knitting in a twist! It originally meant don't act all touchy and temperamental and among men who used it, it carried a connotation of acting in a dizzy, feminine manner. The expression now includes the sub-text of being confused and not knowing what to do. The expression was in fairly wide use from 1950 onwards, and it had a kind of boldness about it, actually mentioning women's undergarments out loud.

Strangely, knickers has slowly come to mean undergarments, both male and female, which are small and tight. (If we want to mention big ones, we say boxer shorts or bloomers.)

Knickers said as an expression of contempt and disbelief came later. People say it when they either don't agree with someone or don't believe them. Nobody really knows why, but it was printed in *The Times* in 1971 and has been fairly common ever since.

What is the origin of the expression *tying the knot* when people get married?

There's the fairly obvious symbolism of two people entering a binding contract, thus metaphorically tying a knot, and in recent times the expression has proven to be apt because there is always some way of untying a knot.

The phrase has, however, more than likely developed from the 400-year-old practice called a true lovers' knot: a complex thing involving two interlacing bows, but with only two ends left dangling. (You can't fake it by joining two existing bows together because then you'd have four ends dangling.)

But the origin of the lovers' knot goes a long way back in time, much further than the 16th century, to ancient Rome before, and also to classical Greece, where the legendary figure of Mercury or Hermes was messenger to the gods. He carried a staff of office that was originally believed to have been a straight stick around which were twined two ribbons. These were twined in the same way as those on the girdle of a bride, hence the association of knotted ribbons with affection. Later, the ribbons on Mercury's staff were replaced by a pair of snakes but the lovers' knot symbolism continued.

 Why do all Mozart's compositions have a *Köchel* number?

Mozart composed an unbelievably huge amount of material, but he was haphazard and didn't organise things very well. Towards the end of his life he was terribly poor and just lived from one commission to the next, eventually dying at 35 as a total pauper and being buried in an unmarked grave. Naturally there was no inventory of his works left in the estate because there was no estate.

At that time people weren't showing much interest in Mozart, and his compositions were scattered all over Europe. They might never have been fully recovered if it hadn't been for Ludwig Ritter von Köchel. He was an Austrian botanist with an immense admiration for the music of Mozart and, accustomed as he was to classifying things, he took on the enormous task of collecting, ordering and numbering all Mozart's music. (His catalogue was published in 1862.) So Köchel numbers are usually attached to anything you hear or see of Mozart. Often Köchel's name is reduced to K, followed by the number. A radio announcement or a CD cover or a concert advertisement often gives the title, then the letter K and the number: Mozart, Mass in C Minor, K. 139.

Köchel died in 1877, having done a classification job that made him famous for ever more.

Q How did the name *Ku Klux Klan* come about?

The Klan started operating in Tennessee in 1866, at the end of the Civil War, with a leader called the Grand Wizard. The organisation was Anti-Negro, anti-Catholic, anti-Jewish, and anti-foreign.

Ninety-nine out of 100 sources will tell you that the name derives from the Greek word *kuklos*, meaning circle. That word survives in English in all sort of words: cycle, bicycle and even the flower cyclamen. The Ku Klux people added the word Klan and continued the fanciful nomenclature by having *k*averns which held *k*onvocations presided over by a *k*alif. Regional commanders were called Cyclops, presumably from the legendary Greek one-eyed monster.

The characteristic white hoods Klansmen wore were partly so they couldn't be identified. Their headgear is distantly related to the Spanish hoods worn in Andalusia by extremely Christian men at the time of Easter, but they are usually black.

Despite being ordered by the Grand Wizard to disband in 1869, and laws passed against it in 1870 and 1871, the Ku Klux Klan remained active and went underground. It began again in 1915 and has had various resurgences from the 1920s onwards.

There is a fairly unsubstantiated theory that the name comes from the sound of a rifle being loaded and cocked. But most autho-rative sources say the name comes from the Greek word for circle.

**Do *lamingtons* have anything to do
with *Leamington Spa*?**

No. The spa town is spelt and pronounced differently from the
cakes: the spa is pronounced 'Lemmington'.

The little cakes, I understand, were invented in Australia, and
named after the Governor of New South Wales in 1896 who was
Lord Lamington. He was only 36 and keen on sports. The
Australians came to like him very much, and the relaxed way in
which he mixed with everybody. Round about then, someone
invented a chocolate-coated sponge square rolled in grated
coconut (the origins are mysterious) and it is believed that, because
of his popularity, the confection was named after the governor
and the lamington was born.

Lord Lamington may even have been flattered to have a cake
named after him but it must have made life difficult for his
descendants. Imagine — every time the following Lords
Lamington met an Australian or New Zealander there would be
endless jokes about chocolate and coconut. That problem solved
itself in 1951 when the last Lord Lamington died.

Where does the word *lampoon* come from?

A lampoon is a personal satire that is scurrilous and
ridiculous. It is believed to be derived from *lampons*, a 17th-century
French vernacular word for let's drink or everyone drink up, often
used in the chorus of drinking songs — and drinking songs have
never been noted for their politeness or sensitivity.

What is the explanation for the expression
laugh one's socks off?

There are many expressions involving laughter: laughing in someone's face, laughing like a drain, being laughed out of court, making someone laugh on the other side of their face, having the last laugh.

But laughing your socks off is not really an example of these. It is the colloquial use of a verb intensifier. Because socks are quite tricky to get on, saying that something knocked them off makes the action you're describing more vivid — it intensifies the verb.

That particular intensifier is very variable, and isn't confined to laughing. You will also hear it said that a sports team beat the socks off the opposition, a high price in a shop will shock the socks off someone and some unfortunate people are said to bore the socks off everyone.

 What is a *laughing jackass*?

Properly, a jackass is another word for a male donkey: jack meaning male. Since about 1830 the word had laughing attached to it, to mean a stupid ignorant fellow. And in 19th-century Australia the term laughing jackass was used to mean the kookaburra, a very noisy bird with a rapid shouting cry like an insane laugh.

Nineteenth-century New Zealand had no kookaburras and very few donkeys, but the term was used here as early as 1860 to describe a species of owl that laughs, and some noisy seabirds. Somewhere, somehow the term ceased to describe birds and is now used mainly to describe people who are irritatingly noisy.

 Why are certain kinds of political leanings described as *left* and others as *right*?

At the end of the 18th century, France altered its method of rule, and the king had to accept a National Assembly. When this met, for no reason anyone knows, the progressive and radical members used to gather and sit on the left side of the king, and their opponents, the reactionaries, sat on the right.

The description left and right gradually came to describe those two political factions. Oddly enough, the terms didn't become common in English until about 1920, when they began to seem appropriate in describing the Spanish Civil War and the rise of Fascism and Nazism. The American political system doesn't feel comfortable with the terms, and they're seldom used there.

 Why are Roman Catholics sometimes referred to as *left-footers*?

Since ancient Roman times left has often been regarded as slightly sinister, unlucky, a bad omen. (The word sinister is from the old Latin word for left.)

In ancient Rome it was considered unlucky to enter a house with the left foot first, and a servant was employed to make sure all visitors put their right foot through the door first. (That is the origin of the term footman.) So to call Roman Catholics left-footers indicated that there was something odd and strange — even sinister — about them.

The specific expression left-footer concerning Catholics is believed to come from Ireland, based on the observation that the right foot is the logical one to drive a spade into the ground, and using the left foot was distinctly odd. Hence, a left-footer was someone who was unusual, out of kilter.

Q **Does a person have to be dead to be a *legend*?**

According to a selection of dictionaries, it is not wrong to describe a person as a legend while they're still alive. It's true that the word carries a connotation that whatever it was happened years ago and may have attained some mythical qualities but there's no stated requirement to be dead.

The general definition of a legendary person is a person whose fame or notoriety makes them a source of exaggerated and romanticised tales and exploits. By the mid-20th century, the word legend was commonly used to refer to a very famous or notorious person.

Q **When someone is easily beaten we say that we *licked them hollow*. Why?**

In early English, lick meant thrash or beat and some of that meaning still survives. In the 16th century you find the expression to lick whole meaning completely, and by the 17th century you sometimes find to beat hollow.

The actual phrase — to lick hollow — doesn't crop up in scholarly sources, but I consider it very likely that the derivation must come from those two threads of meaning: to lick whole, meaning completely. The pronunciation of whole somehow became modified over the years to hollow, but the meaning remains as it originally was.

Q **What is the meaning of the phrase *as sure as God made little green apples*?**

It's a very old American expression meaning that something is certain and definite. The saying might transgress Christian-Judaic beliefs, in that Christians and Jews would surely believe that God must be credited with making considerably more than just apples. This, of course, is exactly what the expression *does* reinforce — that God made everything, including sour things like little green apples!

Recently there has been some confusion about this expression because of a popular song that said 'God *didn't* make little green apples' but you have to listen to the lyrics carefully to realise that the negative is deliberate: 'If that's not loving you, then all I have to say is God didn't make little green apples, and it don't rain in Indianapolis in the summertime . . . .'.

Living the life of Reilly: **who was Reilly, and what sort of life did he live?**

He lived luxuriously and comfortably — that's what the expression means. This particular Reilly is believed to be an example of just how powerful and memorable a character from a popular song can be, like the man who broke the bank at Monte Carlo or Mrs Worthington who was advised not to put her daughter on the stage.

The song thought to have inspired this expression is about a man whose name was actually O'Reilly but who was completely fictional. He was spelt originally as Reilly although in modern times you sometimes see it as Riley.

There was a popular vaudeville artist called Pat Rooney who sang the song 'Are You the O'Reilly?' to enormous effect during the latter half of the 19th century. The song was so well known that the audience used to join in each chorus, which went:

> Are you the O'Reilly who keeps this hotel?
> Are you the O'Reilly they speak of so well?
> Are you the O'Reilly they speak of so highly?
> Gor blimey O'Reilly . . . you're looking well.

From this song it is believed the expression life of Reilly went into popular parlance.

In 1919 we see the expression appearing, this time in another song:

> Faith and my name is Kelly, Michael Kelly
> But I'm living the life of Reilly just the same.

 Are *lounge lizards* always male?

When the expression was first printed in the United States in 1923 it meant sleek adventurous men who frequented places where elegant women gather in expectation of their money and their caresses.

There *is* a female version, lounge lizzies, which came from Australia in the 1920s but the meaning is different: writers of gossip columns or social chit-chat. Normally lounge lizards are male.

Q When a thing is neither hot nor cold, why do we say it is *lukewarm*?

We're actually saying the same thing twice: *luke* is believed to be from the 11th-century English word *hleow*, meaning warm.

Q Is the *luna rossa* a genuine astronomical phenomenon?

Yes, it is, though perhaps properly described as a weather phenomenon rather than an astronomical one. *Luna rossa* means red moon. I am told that this only happens very occasionally in New Zealand because there needs to be real heat in the sun during the day. Sometimes, in the heat of an Italian summer, the moon at night has a reddish tint — it is a *luna rossa*. And it signifies that the summer heat is not going to go away just yet.

Unlike the phrase blue moon, which has an idiomatic significance in English, the phrase red moon doesn't seem to have any comparative significance in Italian, though Italian people will sometimes say *luna rossa stasera, domani sera bella*: there is a red moon tonight, so tomorrow will be wonderful. It has a faint similarity to the English phrase Red sky at night, shepherd's delight.

The song 'Luna Rossa' is very well known, and it also has an air of romance, warmth, happiness, hope and good weather.

Q What is a *lupin pooter*?

It's a character in a well-known book, *The Diary of a Nobody* by George and Weedon Grossmith, published in 1892. It's all about a very ordinary man in an ordinary suburb with an ordinary job, and yet somehow the book is terribly funny. The main character is Mr Charles Pooter, who has a son called Lupin. So Lupin Pooter is the 'nobody's' child!

Why do we sometimes say something is
the real McCoy?

There are two very similar expressions with slightly different origins: the real McCoy and the real McKay.

Language scholar Eric Partridge believes that the expression real McKay originated in Scotland late in the 19th century, where it was believed to describe a particularly good whisky, and the expression was also widely used to describe people of excellent qualities. Scottish whisky was exported to the United States, where people of Scottish origin drank it and kept the expression alive.

But there is a twist. In 1867 a young livestock breeder called Joseph McCoy bought some land in Kansas and offered generous prices for longhorn buffalo. The catch was that the herds had to be driven on a trek three months long. Many drivers stuck this out and delivered buffalo to him. In his first four years over two million animals made the long trek to McCoy's yards, and because he stuck to his word and paid attractive prices, the livestock fraternity used the expression the real McCoy to describe a situation that was honest. Alistair Cook says that McCoy was one of the rare American promoters whose production exceeded his propaganda.

To reinforce the use of the expression, there rose into prominence an American boxer called Kid McCoy who was very successful towards the end of the century. The cowboys' phrase real McCoy was frequently applied to the boxer. So the phrase real McCoy became wedged into the American language, though you still occasionally hear someone of British origin say the real McKay.

Q Is there any reason why *Magdalen* College at Oxford University is pronounced *maudlin*?

There is a character in the New Testament called Mary, who came from the village of Magdala on the shores of Lake Tiberius. In the custom of the time, she was referred to as Mary of Magdala, or Mary the Magdalena. When the New Testament went into English, her name retained the Latin form, Magdalene.

But in parallel, Mary Magdalene had become a very big deal in France: there is a somewhat unsubstantiated belief that she actually died there. But certainly her name was used in many religious places in France, in the form of an ancient French variation written as Madeleine. The figure of Mary Magdalene was also popular in England where 200 ancient churches were dedicated to her.

Various versions of the French vernacular pronunciation drifted into English, with the g sound rather glossed over into an aa-oo sound, and eventually into an aw sound. We must remember that this is a time in history when not everybody could write, and of those who could write, not everybody could spell. (Shakespeare's spelling was often wayward, even when he wrote his own name.) So various versions of many words floated around, often in quite respectable circumstances. When Chaucer used the name of Mary Magdalene three times he spelt it three different ways — and two of those echoed the vernacular French pronunciation, Mawdelayne.

Chaucer died in 1400 and Magdalen College was established just 58 years later, in 1458, when there were at least four different ways of spelling Mary Magdalene in English, though the pronunciation was fairly standard as Mary Mawdlen.

The clerk who drafted the original charter for the college, in English, read the official name as Maria Magdalene — the full, formal Latin name is Collegium Beatae Mariae Magdalene — but he wrote down Maudlyn which, with its ancient French origins, was the way ordinary English people said the word. The college has a letter from King Henry VII himself which uses the Latin spelling and letters from the reign of King Henry VIII using various spellings — Magdalene and also Mawdlin. But it was the ancient *pronunciation* that survived, side by side with the equally ancient Latin spelling.

There is a total lack of consistency in this explanation in that other places in England named after Mary Magdalene are written and pronounced Magdalene. Oxford University's Magdalen College prefers to stick to the pronunciation that was the norm in mediaeval times.

(A single consonant is quite often dropped in the pronunciation of an English word . . . e.g. we write down knitting but say nitting, and then we say nite and write down night. It's quite common, so the G was dropped from the pronunciation of poor old Mary Magdalene, first in French where she became Madeleine and then in English where she became 'Mawdlen'.)

 Has the expression *the mark of Cain* changed its meaning?

The phrase comes straight from Genesis but there are actually two different expressions derived from the same Bible story.

The Bible says that the mark of Cain protected him from being killed. But, besides that mark, Cain also carried a curse which meant that he had to wander all his life.

People in contemporary times sometimes confuse the two and say one when they mean the other. An actor said in an interview that after he left a long-term role in a television serial, nobody would employ him — it was as if he had the mark of Cain upon him. That situation is not, in fact, either the mark of Cain or the curse of Cain, according to the biblical derivation, but both terms are nowadays used carelessly to mean carrying some sort of stigma that everyone knows about.

Marmite and *Vegemite* — what actually are they?

Marmite originated in England about 1900, and was imported into New Zealand until 1930. During the 1940s, New Zealand started manufacturing its own. Manufacturers encouraged the illusion that it was an extract of meat, but actually it is made only from vegetables. The name is the French word for a stockpot or cooking pot.

Vegemite, invented in Melbourne in 1923, uses a yeast paste from a brewery, with an extract of celery and onions. Originally it was called Parwill but this didn't catch on, so a competition was held among the public, and the name Vegemite won. Imported into New Zealand until 1957, it has been manufactured here since 1958.

Why does *maudlin* mean tearful and sad?

Nothing much is known for certain about Mary Magdalene but that didn't stop people deciding things about her, and a legend developed that she had been a woman of easy virtue before she became repentant, reflecting on the sadnesses in her life and weeping a lot. So painters often depicted her as a tearful woman. This was during the period when the g was dropped in pronouncing her name, so the word Mawdlen came to describe someone, or something, which was always sad and weeping.

It still does mean that, but the spelling of the word has followed the pronunciation, so it is written, and spoken as maudlin, unlike the Oxford college of Magdalen, which is pronounced the same way but sticks with the original spelling of Mary's name.

In past centuries women who had fallen from grace were referred to as mawdelens, and some institutions that looked after such women, and sometimes their babies as well, were known as Mawdlens.

Mary was eventually canonised: she is the patron saint of repentant sinners and those who follow a contemplative life. Her feast day is 22 July.

What is the origin of the distress call *mayday*?

It's French, the word *aidez* meaning help, with m' in front, meaning help me. In 1927 the International Radio Telegraph Convention adopted this as the international signal for distress, and in English-speaking countries the spelling has become phonetic: mayday.

 Why is a military dining room called a *mess*?

This originates in the Latin word *missus*, meaning to place out, later influenced by the French word *mettre*, to place (food). The short version mess came to mean a group of people, usually four, who sat together and were served from the same dishes.

Shakespeare uses it in *Love's Labour's Lost* — 'You three fools lack'd me fool to make up the mess'. The meaning of four people being served as a separate group evolved into seatings of people of some privilege, hence military officers.

The word mess is now sometimes used more generally to mean a kind of eating room for everyone.

Q **Why are Catholics sometimes called *Micky Doolans*?**

Whether Micky Doolan was ever a real person or not, he sounds very Irish and since the middle of the 19th century this name has been in common use as a slang term for a Roman Catholic, in a satirical reference to the fact that many Irish people are Roman Catholic. It is heard in various forms: sometimes just Doolan by itself, and sometimes just Micky by itself, or shortened to a Mick.

What is the origin of the practice of putting *milk into teacups before the tea*?

Tea came to England at the same time as Chinese porcelain, which was very strong, but because the new drink required teapots and teacups, which were shapes not seen in England before, the English ceramicists had to learn to copy these shapes — and those early English pots and cups *did* crack if they came into contact with something too hot.

Hence the English developed the custom of swirling hot-ish water around in the pot to warm it, before pouring in the boiling water, and of putting milk into the cup before the hot tea went in. This was a well-established practice by the end of the 18th century. By the 19th century there was probably no need since English ceramics had improved.

Interestingly, people who have milk or cream in coffee almost always put it in *after* the hot liquid.

 Non-Christian countries may not necessarily notice the Christian *millennium*. Why?

The Christian millennium doesn't match up at all with the calendar systems used in other cultures.

In the Muslim calendar, 2000 is 1421 and in Iran that year is 1379. In Nepal, where the calendar system is way past its second thousand, they had a millennium back in 1943. Buddhist countries like Thailand see 2000 as the year 2543 and in the Jewish calendar it is 5760 in 2000. But Japan counts its official years from the start of an emperor's reign, so 2000 was year 12 there.

 Why is the record of a meeting called the *minutes* when the meeting may have taken several hours? Is there any relation to minutes on a clock?

In a vague kind of way, there is. When you say that someone takes the minutes at a meeting, you are using the abbreviated form of an old Latin phrase, *minuta scriptura*, which means writing of the small details. Eventually the words became reduced to one word — minutes — and the meaning enlarged slightly to its present use which is a summary of all transactions, taking care to be exact about important details.

The minutes on a clock come from the same source, the Latin *minutus*, meaning small, which eventually gives us minute, a small part of an hour, and, by way of French, min*ute*, meaning very small.

 Is the Scottish version of Menzies —
Mingies **— correct?**

Yes, it is correct. In very old Scotland there used to be a written symbol rather like a squiggly figure 3, which was used to write down a sound called a palatal, which is a kind of ny sound. When people tried to write these words into English, there was no equivalent to this sqiggly 3 and so they wrote down a z because the old symbol looked a bit like that letter. When English-speaking people saw the z, they pronounced the word wrongly.

Thus, the Scottish name which is correctly pronounced Mingis became written down in English as Menzies. But a true Scot will still prefer that it is said as Mingis.

Similarly Dalziel: the z shouldn't really be there, and this name can variously be pronounced as De-ell (as in the television police dramas featuring Dalziel and Pascoe) or Dalyeel.

Q **Where does the word** *moniker* **come from?**

The meaning of the word is fairly clear — an informal or slang way of describing your name. It is spelt various ways and the origin of the word is very mysterious.

Most scholars agree that it developed out of hobo or tramp talk in the 19th century. Some believe it is a corruption of the Latin word *monogramma* which also is a sign of identity. Others think it might be a corruption of monitor, which comes from the Latin *monere*, meaning to advise.

And another school of thought is that it's a jokey tramp version of the word monk, since tramps sometimes joked about their solitary all-male existence and said they lived like monks.

One scholar is of the opinion that the word moniker is a slang result of not-very-well educated people making a slang word by combining monogram and signature.

Q **Why is a *monkfish* so called?**

The name of this deep-dwelling fish, often described as a kind of shark, is a bit of a worry, because it's been called that for a very long time, and there are several theories about why.

(1) Some people think its misshapen head does have a fanciful resemblance to a monk wearing a cowl.

(2) Because of the way its head is made, it can appear to be gazing upwards — star-gazing — which contributed to the image of a monk in prayer. Indeed, the fish is sometimes called the *stargazer*.

(3) Apparently when you see the fish in the water, it is brown and flaps about a bit, looking somewhat like the robes of a monk (not the head).

(4) It is believed that way back in mediaeval times monks in monasteries who didn't eat meat on some days, actually liked this better than other fish, so it came to be called monk's fish.

Monkfish is eaten quite a lot. One food expert says it has very firm flesh that cooks to a pleasant sweet taste, which is why the monkfish is sometimes called 'poor man's lobster' and in many places the monkfish's liver is regarded as very desirable.

It's called many other things too: angler fish, bulldog fish, toadfish, goosefish or angel shark. In early New Zealand, the fish was sometimes but rarely called Maori chief fish. And it is sometimes sold under the semi-attractive name deep sea cod, though it's much closer to shark.

The fish looks so bad that in parts of Scandinavia and Iceland, it is considered a joke to feed tourists a delicious dish of monkfish, and then, after they've finished, show them a picture of what they've just eaten. It is so ugly that for many years people who hadn't seen it believed it was only a fantasy and Mary Queen of Scots embroidered little pictures of it alongside things like unicorns, believing that both didn't really exist.

 Why is part of a ship known as the *monkey island*?

It's the small deck above the wheelhouse. If a compass is surrounded with steel its efficiency is affected so on a steel ship the compass is mounted above the wheelhouse (and sometimes you even need to use magnets as compass adjusters because the steel is still fairly close).

Iron started being used in ships late in the 19th century and then steel in the 20th century, so the need to place the compass out of range is, in naval terms, fairly recent, as is the term monkey island.

You might have to climb as many as three ladders to get to the wheelhouse, and the monkey island was one more ladder up, so there could be a total of four ladders to climb. Among seamen, the word monkey was sometimes used to describe places that were awkward to get to, so although there is no formal derivation to be found the name, like crow's nest, probably has a fairly obvious origin — reaching the monkey island required some agility and when you got there it was very high.

 What is the meaning of the phrase *having a monkey on your back*?

This usually refers to some other kind of persistent problem that clings and won't go away, like having an albatross around your neck (Coleridge in *Ancient Mariner*) or a cross to bear (New Testament).

But the expression is often used also to mean having a drug habit: a persistent gnawing feeling that you must have a drug fix. Or it can mean something quite respectable, like a long mortgage.

 Is it *moot point* or a *mute point*?

The two words are entirely different.

Moot is often used as a legal term, and means open to debate or argument. It comes from a very old German word *muoze*, meaning a meeting, which became the Anglo-Saxon *mot*.

Mute comes from the Latin *mutus*, meaning silent, so its meaning is really the opposite of moot because debate and argument invariably involve talking, while to be mute is to make no sound at all.

 Why does *mountebank* mean a charlatan or a conman?

It's Italian from *montambanco* which in turn comes from *monter banco*, to climb onto a bench. So it means a person who climbs up on a stage to sell something or attract crowds by tricks or oratory — a seller of fake medicines. The word means exactly the same in English, and has developed the spelling and pronunciation mountebank.

 What is the origin of *mud in your eye*?

There are two possibilities. It may be a First World War expression: to the soldiers on the battlefield, having mud in your eye was considered more desirable than blood, or worse. It is also possible that this is a racing expression: when a horse puts mud in another horse's eye, it is because the first horse is running faster!

Why is the word *mufti* used to describe plain or civilian clothes as opposed to uniform?

The word is Arabic and means a legal ruling within the Muslim faith, or a religious official who has the right to rule on a point of Muslim law.

During the 19th century, there was a fashion for British military officers, when off duty, to wear elaborate dressing gowns and tasselled smoking caps. These vaguely resembled the actual religious robes of a Muslim leader, so it is believed that the practice grew of referring to the officers as being in mufti, and the word passed into English to mean off-duty clothes, rather than official uniform.

Q **Where does the expression *mum's the word* originate?**

It's very old — between 16th and 17th centuries. Mum means remaining silent and it has meant that from at least 1500 onwards. The word is believed to be simply an imitation of keeping the lips closed, a phonogram. Extending the word mum into the expression mum's the word didn't really take off until about 1850 and because mum is a word meaning silence, the saying mum's the word could, I suppose, be categorised as an anti-phonogramic paradox.

There is another expression in English that seems to be related to mum's the word and actually means the same thing. My lips are sealed is much more recent: it's believed to have started as a misreporting of a remark by British Prime Minister Stanley Baldwin. Sometime in 1935 he was asked a trick question and replied, 'My lips are not yet unsealed.' This was a double negative so in the interests of economy of printing space, most reporters wrote that he had said, 'My lips are sealed.' This abbreviated version became the norm and has been widely used since.

Mum also developed another meaning rather by accident: a shortened form of mummy, a children's word for their mother. This also didn't come into use until probably the late 19th century.

Mum has taken on in a big way, and now has various shades of connotation of affection.

Q **What is the origin of the term *mumbo-jumbo*?**

Mumbo-jumbo is from an African Mandingo word, *mama dyumbo*. It is the name of a custom for keeping disorderly wives in order: a man disguised as a grotesque idol makes hideous noises at night, and causes a crowd to gather, upon which the woman is stripped naked in front of them, and whipped by the grotesque.

The word was brought out of Africa by the famous Scottish explorer Mungo Park, who used it in his book *Travels in the Interior of Africa*, published in the late 18th century.

Over the years, the term has come to mean blind unreasoning worship, or sometimes a description of words that seem meaningless to someone who doesn't understand.

Q **What is the difference between a *myth* and a *legend*?**

Quite often they seem interchangeable.

A legend is an account of something notable that happened in history, and has become a traditional tale. Sometimes it is not an authentic story, but is popularly regarded as true; sometimes it *is* an authentic story.

Legend can also describe a person whose exploits, either good or bad, are widely known, and that person is sometimes regarded as real, like Robin Hood, or sometimes unreal, like Hercules. On this basis of good and bad exploits, Caligula and Hitler can be described as legendary, but so can Sir Edmund Hillary and Mother Teresa.

On the other hand a myth is a traditional story, but usually fictitious and often involving the supernatural (that's important) and often provides an explanation for a natural or social phenomenon or a religious belief.

With some caution here we could point to the story of Maui

fishing up the whole North Island: it's a traditional, widely told story that explains a natural state of affairs and involves supernatural powers.

A good way of remembering the two definitions is to think of Santa Claus. He is a myth based on a legend because Saint Nicholas was a real Turkish person, widely known for centuries after his death. He became a legend, but he didn't ride reindeer through the sky at night. That's a myth.

In general myths are easier to scorn than legends, which is probably why, in modern times, the word myth has taken on a shade of meaning that something is widely believed but is not true.

Q **What does *in the necessary* mean?**

This word was in use until the end of the 19th century, meaning the lavatory. There was an old rule that 'If two persons are known to be in the necessary together they shall be fined'. So if two people were found in the loo at the same time, they were in trouble.

Q **Is to throw someone out *neck and crop* related to the other expression *to come a cropper*?**

Brewer says the two expressions are related, Collins says they're not, believing that come a cropper derives from the word crupper, a belt that holds horse saddlery in the right place: if it loosens, you fall off.

Neck and crop means completely, fully, so if you come a cropper you fall badly. Crop is also quite an important part of a bird's internal workings: without its neck and crop, a bird would be completely useless. There also used to be an old punishment of thrusting someone into a cage with their chin and knees tightly forced together, and from that came the phrase neck and heels.

It's possible that neck and crop and neck and heels are somehow related, but the only truthful answer is that nobody's sure.

 Q **Why are *Neenish tarts* so called and where did the name come from?**

These small tarts filled with a sweet creamy mixture, and iced half with vanilla and half with chocolate, are apparently completely unknown outside Australasia. Angus & Robertson's text on patisserie says they are believed to have been invented in the outback of Australia. Considering what they're made of, the outback connection doesn't seem likely, but the Australian connection seems to stick.

The word arose in Australia, possibly as a corruption of a German word, though it isn't clear which one. An Australian researcher discovered a letter written in the early 1920s that referred to 'Neinisch cakes, made of mother's German pastry'. The word Neinisch also appears in *Mrs Drake's Home Cookery* book published in Australia in 1929, in a recipe for Neinisch cake.

But the word Neinisch means nothing in German; it is not a real word. By the late 1930s the word Neinisch was still being used in Australia, to describe cakes that were sometimes pink and white; they settled into brown and white later.

There seems to have been two changeovers of the spelling. After the 1920s they started being referred to as Nienisch tarts, but this doesn't make sense in German either — there is no such word. By 1955 there had been another spelling change — the *Edmonds Cookbook* in New Zealand contained the recipe, as Neenish tarts.

So the sad answer is that scholars can't make up their minds about where the name came from.

Q Why is a British village called *New Zealand*?

New Zealand is the name of a little hamlet in Wiltshire. It doesn't appear in the *Oxford Dictionary of English Place Names* — apparently it's too small. It is in a very remote part of the county, and was named about the same time as Britain became aware of the country of New Zealand, because they were both perceived as being a very long way away!

There is also a part of Salisbury Plain that is called New Zealand Farm — for the same reason. This could cause a problem for genealogists if someone's documentation says they were 'born in New Zealand'.

Q **Does the expression *next of kin* include in-laws?**

Kin comes into English from the German word *Kind*, child, which itself comes from the Latin *genus*, same kind. Strictly, kin means people to whom you are related by blood: the *Oxford Dictionary* defines kin as people with a common ancestor.

Kith has its ancestry in the German word *Kund*, meaning known and identifiable, and refers to friends and acquaintances.

In general conversation kin can mean the whole family, including in-laws. But usually in legal matters and the inheriting of titles or money it is likely to be blood only. Insurance companies and hospitals may allow a spouse to be next of kin.

Q **Why do certain men's names almost automatically have *nicknames* attached to them? Why is a man named Wilson always called Tug?**

Young men who'd had to work hard to get into a good college — they weren't rich or well connected but had to sit term exams and apply themselves — were correctly called collegers, but they were known as tugs, which is believed to be short for toga, probably indicating a devotion to classical study instead of pleasure. Somewhere in the 19th century the word tug became attached to a man called Wilson, nobody is sure who, and it stuck.

A man called Palmer is often nicknamed Peddler Palmer.

The word peddler is related to the old word palmer meaning a pilgrim who carried a palm leaf as a sign that he or she had been to the Holy Land, but it was also used to describe a trickster who could put money down on the counter of a shop, take the goods and somehow sneak back some of the money — in their palm. The two words became associated so that anyone called Palmer was often nicknamed Peddler.

Any man called Miller is usually known as Dusty Miller.

This one is self-evident.

Someone with the name Clark is always known as Nobby.

To the historical working classes, the profession of clerk was thought to be learned and literate, and since the nobility were also thought to be learned and literate, the nickname Nobby became attached to anyone who *worked* as a clerk, and then later to anyone *called* Clark.

People called Martin are often called Pincher Martin.

He was a real person in the 19th century, Admiral Sir William Martin — a strict disciplinarian who was constantly having ratings pinched for minor offences. Hence the name for him — and later everyone else — Pincher Martin.

Why are men called *Robert, Richard, Henry and Edward* usually known as *Bob, Dick, Harry and Ted* when the short version appears to have little connection with the original?

There is no rational answer to this. Robert is a French name originating in Germany and has several diminutives: Rob, Robbie, Bob, Bobby. The short form, Rob, used to be Hob or Dob, which has now vanished. Richard also is an old French name from German, and has become Rick and Dick. Edward, an old English name acquired later by other languages, has become Ed, Eddie, Ned or Ted.

Henry is the other way round — it's a Germanic name, and it used to be Harry, which was the formal version. Round about the 17th century Harry somehow became informal and Henry slipped into being the formal version.

Shortened alterations still happen in modern times: in Australia especially Barry becomes Baz and Gary becomes Gazza.

Q **Why are bad dreams called *nightmares*?**

It's a very old expression and it has nothing to do with horses. For many centuries there was a belief that a special kind of evil spirit went around waiting for people to sleep and then settling on their prone bodies and sending evil waves into their unconscious minds. In Latin this creature was called an incubus, an evil spirit that smothers you, from the Latin *incubare*, to lie on — as in the modern word incubate.

But strangely enough, although the English believed in this night-time spirit, the English language for once didn't borrow the Latin word but used an Old Norse word, *maera*, which also means an evil spirit that smothers you. Gradually the pronunciation turned it into a nightmare and 99 per cent of people forgot that the ancient word *maera* meant a frightening invisible spirit.

 Where does the word *norks* come from?

This expression for breasts is Australian, and it is believed to have originated in a 1950s Norco Dairy company butter wrapper showing a cow with a very big udder. The word was introduced into common parlance by Barry Humphries, in the guise of hoon Barry McKenzie. It first appeared in serious print in 1962.

Q *Nothing venture, nothing win* **is part of Sir Edmund Hillary's coat-of-arms. Shouldn't it be *Nothing ventured, nothing won*?**

This is a version of a phrase that is extraordinarily old. In Latin it dates right back to 100 years before Jesus, then through Chaucer in 1390 as 'Who that nought dare undertake, By right he shall no profit make'.

By 1523, the phrase had modified into 'He that nothing adventureth, nothing getteth'. Throughout the early 17th century it underwent a few more changes, sometimes 'Nothing dare, nothing achieve', 'nothing venture, nothing have' or 'nought venture, nought have'. Shakespeare used a version of it, and in the hands of Sir Charles Sedley in 1668 it became 'Nothing venture, nothing win', which seems to have stuck.

The version used by Sir Edmund isn't actually wrong; it's an example of a grammatical device called ellipsis or omission: the leaving out of a few bits because everyone understands that they should be there so there's no need to say them. We do it all the time.

Mottos are usually as brief as possible. So, in the interests of brevity, this motto, which should read 'If you have ventured nothing, then you can only win nothing', has been reduced to 'Nothing venture, nothing win'.

Interestingly, another version, 'Who dares wins', is the motto of the SAS.

Q | **What lies behind the expression *to the nth degree*?**

It means to the ultimate or, as Shirley Maddock had it in one of her book titles, 'far as man may go'. The expression comes from mathematics, where the letter n is used as a symbol denoting an indefinite number.

So if you say, for instance, 'The catering at the wedding was meticulous to the nth degree', you mean that it wasn't just good, or excellent, but absolutely beyond expectation to an indefinite level — like the mathematical symbol n.

Q **Where does *the expression OK* or *okay* come from?**

Absolutely nobody knows for sure where it came from. Scholars and researchers have come up with 16 different versions of where the expression comes from, including suggested derivations from expressions that sound roughly similar in languages ranging from Scottish, Norwegian, Burmese and German to American Indian, Finnish, French and Greek, but the truth is no one knows for sure.

Q **Why are non-drinkers *on the wagon*?**

The expression dates back to the United States in the 1890s, when the dust in cities was kept under control by carts carrying water, which was sprinkled on the streets. People who wanted to slake their thirst on a hot day would climb aboard and have a drink — but of course it was only water. This gave rise to the expression climbing aboard the water cart, which gathered the connotation of deliberately avoiding strong liquor and drinking water instead. By 1901, the expression was in print. Over the following century the expression has settled into slightly different wording, and become on the wagon, but it still means the same.

Q **Why is a person with extensive knowledge said to *know his or her onions*?**

There are two answers to this. An early editor of the *Oxford English Dictionary* was Charles Onions, and people acknowledged his expertise by referring to other people as knowing as much as Onions.

But there is also a belief that it derives from Cockney rhyming slang, where instead of saying a person knew a lot about things, they'd say he knew a lot about onion rings. And in the usual way of rhyming slang, the describing word has gone into the language and the actual rhyming word hasn't.

 Was an *orange* so called because of its colour, or was the colour given its name because it was the same as the fruit?

A curious question indeed. Oranges, the fruit, have been around for a very long time. They are thought to have originated in the tropical regions of Asia and their name goes way, way back to the languages of South and Central India. It appears in Sanskrit as *naranga* and then versions of that word travelled through the Persian language into Arabic and then into Old French before it reached English. The version we know, orange, has been in use in English for 600 years. Considering how old the name of the fruit is I'm guessing the colour is named after the fruit.

 Where does the word *outage* come from?

From the word out, fairly obviously. The word has been around since the 1980s, mainly in the United States, and it has a main meaning of things mysteriously missing after a big shipment, or supplies that have passed through a few hands and now don't seem to be intact.

But it is currently the fashion to use or invent words to make things sound softer and less responsible. A power breakdown, which is what it is, indicates immediately that there has been a mechanical or human problem. But authorities don't like being held responsible, so if you say the word outage it carries a neutral connotation: the lights have gone out all by themselves, nobody did it, nothing broke down. It all just went — out. Hence outage immediately gives the vague idea that nobody's to blame.

Q | **Where are you when you're *over the brush*?**

The full expression is living over the brush, in other words living together as man and wife but not married. It's a very old saying, usually found in the northern part of England, and it's thought that it may have been derived from an even older English saying, to leap over the broomstick or leap over the brush, which meant to go through an unreal or mock ceremony and pretend that you are married. Possibly the couple would quite literally hold hands and jump together over an old broom with a bushy end and declare 'we are married'.

What is a *palindrome*?

A palindrome is a word or phrase that spells the same backwards as it does forwards: bob, Madam I'm Adam; able was I ere I saw Elba . . .

The word comes from ancient Greek — *dromos* meaning a course, like a race-track, and *palin* meaning again — so the word actually means running back again along the same track.

We have a very well-known palindrome in New Zealand, the fine singer Patsy Riggir whose surname spells the same forwards and backwards.

A palindrome is a term used only about words, not about numbers, but it can be used adjectivally, by saying palindromic, so when you come across a group of digits that read the same backwards and forwards — the date 27.9.1972, for instance — you can call it a palindromic number.

 What is the background to the marine signal *pan pan*?

This signal isn't nearly as well known to landlubbers as the distress signal mayday, but it also denotes urgency — asking that the airwaves be kept clear in case a distress signal is imminent. For instance, if a small fire was discovered on a ship the crew would maybe signal pan pan because there could be a problem that might or might not get worse. If the fire did become serious the signal would then be changed to mayday.

These spoken verbal signals date back to the 1920s when actual words started to be used in communications instead of just Morse code. French was adopted as the universal language for such signals — hence mayday (from *m'aidez*) for distress, pan pan for urgency, *securité* for safety messages such as storm warnings.

Pan pan is derived from the French word *panne-panne* which is used to mean a breakdown of the norm: something is wrong but the situation is not yet desperate. If a lift in a big building in France is out of order or being repaired, there'll be a sign up saying *En panne*.

Q Should we say *pant* or *pants*?

They are the same word: both abbreviations for pantaloons, which take their name from the fourth-century Saint Pantaleone, who later became a comic figure. There is no real need to keep the final s on pants, it is just a custom. Pant has been used in the singular in the United States for many years (since 1893) — a pant or sometimes a pants. No strict rule applies.

But you're not likely to hear a slack. Slacks were originally trousers of a loose kind from the Old English *slaec*, meaning loose, which goes way back to Latin *lax* — in English both slack and lax still mean something loose. Nor will you encounter a trouser (from *trews*, itself from Scottish *triubhas* influenced by French *trebus*).

Most things with legs or leg-holes are referred to in the plural: togs, tights, daks, grunds, undies, knickers, drawers. Curiously, in New Zealand we refer to the fly of one's trousers, but the word is plural in Britain. Fly is short for fly front, where one piece of material overlaps the other. It's worth pointing out, too, that trouser legs used to be separate, and when evolution joined them together, the plural was an obvious carry-over. There is a whole list of things with two components which are generally mentioned in plural: scissors, glasses and pliers.

Q *Paparazzi:* **what exactly does it mean?**

It is the plural form of paparazzo, which means a particular breed of freelance photographer who makes a living by taking photos of celebrities in private situations, against their will, and then selling them to newspapers and magazines.

The word originated in the 1960 Fellini movie, *La Dolce Vita*, in which there was a character called Paparazzo, a photographer who specialised in society and show-biz pics. This character, supposedly fictional, was based on a real person, a photographer called Tazio Secchiaroli who used to hang around Rome photographing filmstars and royalty. But the name of the movie character Paparazzo went into the English language very quickly, and within a year people started to refer to nuisance photographers in the plural — paparazzi. And the word has been around ever since.

 Q **Why is a *parka* so called?**

Eskimo is the word used to describe the native inhabitants of Northern Canada, Greenland, Alaska and Eastern Siberia. But within that territory are the Aleutian Islands, whose inhabitants are related to the Eskimos but are a slightly different group.

A common garment in the general area has for a long time been a thigh-length coat with a hood usually made of caribou skin and seal fur. Eskimos and Aleutians and Alaskans protected themselves from the cold with this garment, and coats for women had an extra hood used for wrapping round a baby.

Round about 1930, the design of this jacket moved into the rest of the world, for skiing and general outdoor use, and was known by its Aleutian name — parka, which means skin. In contemporary times, however, the word applies to the design of the garment, rather than the fabric.

Q **Where does the word *parky* come from?**

It's a very old word meaning cold, so old that its origin is lost in the mists of time, but some etymologists believe it is a variation on perky — because the cold weather makes you alert, spirited and jaunty, as opposed to the sleepy, soporific effect of warm weather.

Q **What does *having a Parnell* mean?**

Parnell is a suburb of Auckland and before it was gentrified it was considered a place of poor but independent people of some spirit. Since at least 1916, the phrase *a Parnell shout* meant everyone paying for their own drinks, and this has evolved into having a Parnell, which means being on your own, paying for your own drinks and being independent.

Q **What do Americans mean by *a patsy*?**

The word has been commonly used in the United States since the 19th century to mean someone who is easily deceived, a sucker. The word is believed to be derived from an Italian word *pazzo*, meaning a fool.

Q **Is the *pavlova* an Australian invention rather than a New Zealand one?**

Anna Pavlova danced in New Zealand in 1926 and it took a while for the famous egg-white cake to take her name, but there is plenty of evidence to prove that the famous dessert surfaced here first with that title.

As usual, the way of pinning down how and when things began is to find when they were first published. Australians claim that the pavlova is theirs, because the recipe was published there in

1935. But the highly respected Home Economics Department of Otago University established that it was published here in 1934, in Aunt Daisy's recipe book, in between tomato marmalade and boys boiled pudding. And there was not one but three recipes for different kinds of pavlova.

But lexicographer Harry Orsman has the final word in his massive *New Zealand Dictionary*. Under pavlova, he gives a recipe first published in New Zealand in 1929, and another published in 1933.

To be fair, though, calling a meringue cake by that name is something we hold to be indigenous, but the actual idea of making meringue plus whipped cream is certainly not a New Zealand invention. Marie Antoinette ate exactly that two centuries ago, and French pastrycooks have made something quite similar for years, called *vacherin*.

Incidentally, the word meringue probably originates from the German town of Mehr in Yghen, Saxe Coburg Gotha, where the idea of baking egg whites seems to have originated.

Q Why is a measure of acidity called *pH*?

Acidity and alkalinity are measured by the strength of the amount of hydrogen present in any substance.

The expression pH is German: the p stands for the German word *Potenz* which means force or strength (as it does in English: potency) and the H stands for hydrogen. So *pH* is short for the strength of hydrogen present. The figure 7 is used for pure water so acid solutions have a presence of hydrogen lower than 7, and alkaline solutions have a pH factor higher than 7 — more hydrogen.

First published in Germany in 1909, pH was used worldwide soon after.

What is the origin of *picnic*?

It comes from Old French, where one of the meanings of *piquer* is to pick things up or get things. And *nique*, in Old French, meant something of little value.

As early as 1694 the expression *pique-nique* in French was used to describe an informal meal of small dishes at which one nibbled, or sometimes a meal to which every guest brought some food.

Hence, eventually, we get picnic which, in English, has somehow evolved a connotation of being outdoors, but is still sometimes used for casual eating indoors: 'everything was packed ready to move, so we just picnicked'.

Does the expression *pidgin English* have anything to do with pigeons?

Nothing. It's a term that arose because of the English insistence that everyone should speak to them in English, and this included conducting commerce with Chinese and Indians. Quite often these groups could learn the appropriate words but had difficulty in pronouncing them. For instance, the Chinese had difficulty with the letter b and an interior s, so instead of saying business they said pidginess. In time pidginess became just pidgin and then the word was used to describe a whole dialect that evolved around the Pacific area and in some cases actually became the language of a community.

The term has spread throughout the world and is used to refer to communication in which the basic language is rendered in a lumpy sort of way but manages to be understood — as in pidgin French, pidgin English, pidgin German. There is another word with a very similar meaning, creole, which refers to a language combined from two other languages.

Where does the phrase *piece of cake* come from?

The expression, which means that something is easy, is generally acknowledged as arising from war. The famous etymologist Eric Partridge thinks that it derives from the dance known as the cakewalk, which is cheerful and flowing and jaunty and engenders a feeling of ease in those who are watching. The people judged as the best dancers were traditionally awarded a fancy cake as a prize. Hence, saying something was a cakewalk meant that it was happy and free of stress, and this became condensed over the years into just a piece of cake, especially in war zones when a military assignment turned out to be easier than expected, or was predicted to be easily accomplished.

There is an alternative. Ogden Nash used the phrase in 1936 because he seemed to think that eating a piece of cake was easy and pleasant.

Both explanations have two things in common: they acknowledge that cake is pleasant, and they come from the United States.

What is the explanation for the expression *a pig in a poke*?

Poke is the old word for bag or basket, derived from the French word *poche*. In modern English we don't use the word poke with that meaning, but two versions of the word survive in modern English as pocket and pouch.

A pig in a poke has been in use in English for 400 years. It's believed to have originated in country markets where someone would have for sale a small animal squirming around inside a bag, or poke. Telling his customers it was a piglet, the marketer would sometimes succeed in selling it without the customer actually opening the bag to check that it was a pig. So if you bought a pig in a poke without examining it thoroughly, you could end up with something worthless such as a cat. Hence the meaning: to buy anything important without having thoroughly researched it.

What is the derivation of the word *pillock*?

We are in somewhat delicate territory here. It is a contemptuous expression, usually applied to a man or to a piece of information that is regarded as nonsense.

Pillock dates back to the 14th century, and is a way of referring to male genitals. It combines a shortened version of pills, meaning testicles, with ock. Do I have to elaborate further? This is classified as a vulgarism and I don't know *why* a description of maleness should be utilised as such a dismissal.

Pillock, incidentally, is closely related to the similar expression bollocks, which is really spelt ballocks.

Q Why does the English language customarily change the real names of *places* into anglicised versions of the original?

This is a very common practice; all languages do it all the time. Most languages borrow words from other languages and very often the words they've borrowed are changed in pronunciation and spelling. The same thing happens to the names of places.

For instance, the place we call Vienna isn't called Vienna at all but Wien (hence Wiener schnitzel). There is no such place as Munich; its real name is München. And the place where the Anzacs fought is not called Gallipoli and never has been. There is no place in Turkey called Gallipoli; its real name is Gelebolu and if you go there, that's the signpost you have to follow. The city of Florence is actually Firenze and Japan is actually Nihon.

Maori alters English place names too. Hiruharama south of Ruatoria is Jerusalem, for example, and Atene, on the Whanganui River, is Athens.

Why do we talk about someone *playing gooseberry*?

Like many expressions we use, this one has very obscure origins, so obscure in fact that no absolutely definite answer can be given. But some scholars think that it dates back to a time when many more people lived rurally than they do now, and sexual freedom was rather more narrow. So if two people wanted to get closer together than the social rules allowed, they would go out into the fields to work, taking a trusted third person with them. Often, so it seems, they would be picking gooseberries.

The group of three looked more discreet than just two, and the third person would tactfully go on picking fruit, ignoring whatever antics the other two were up to, hence playing gooseberry.

The odd thing is that, like many expressions, this one has reversed its meaning. Nowadays when you hear about someone playing gooseberry, it usually means that their presence is *preventing* two other people from having fun.

 Why are a garden plant and the graphite inside pencils both called *plumbago*?

The word comes from the Greek *polubdos*, meaning lead. You'll also find the plumb bit in plumb-bob, the weighted cord that surveyors use to get a perfect vertical: the lumpy weight at the bottom is usually lead.

Plumbago is also the name of a family that includes various kinds of flowering plants, sometimes called leadwort. This is believed to be because the flowers resemble the colour of lead.

 A well-known village in England is called Stoke Poges. What does *poges* mean?

England is full of places with strange names. On the cover of the *Oxford Dictionary of English Place Names* is a photo of road signs pointing to Ham and Sandwich.

Stoke is an English word dating back about 12 centuries which means an outlying farmstead, a small secondary settlement or village.

Poges is what is called a manorial affix. It comes from the name of the grand family who lived in the manor nearby during the 13th century. Their name was Le Pugeis and that came after Stoke, to designate *which* Stoke anyone was talking about and eventually Stoke Le Pugeis, the little settlement dominated by the Le Pugeis manor house, became Stoke Poges.

Q | **What is the origin of the term *politically correct*?**

That phrase as we know it seems to have begun in the United States around about 1980 when people started to avoid expressions or actions that could denigrate or offend minorities or people considered to be disadvantaged by gender, race, class, sexual orientation, religious beliefs or disability.

Initially this expression was considered a very good thing and many people could see the sense of modifying what they said so as not to be offensive. In 1991 an American dictionary was published called *The Bias-Free Word Finder* which was supposed to help you find politically correct terminology to replace the offensive words you might have used before.

But since 1991 the expression has had a more or less complete reversal of intent. Unfortunately, the enthusiasm for being correct started to get out of hand. For instance, traditional phrases such as 'the right hand of God' were republished as 'the mighty hand of God' in case the traditional version offended left-handed people. And people started being jokey about political correctness — such as wondering how you would describe a Catholic in a wheelchair wearing a fur coat.

Nowadays many people find it difficult to take political correctness seriously because it seems to have gone too far and it's becoming hard to sort out which are the genuine politically correct words that have slid into the language, and which are the jokey ones that people have made up: crippled (disabled, different abilities), jungle (rainforest), janitor (maintenance engineer), short (vertically challenged).

 Is there any connection between *polka* and *polka dots*?

The polka dance originates from Czechoslovakia, where the word *pul* means half and *pul-ka* means a half-step — that little bounce you do in a polka. Polka dots are the regularly spaced spots of the same size that appear on fabric.

A connection between dots and the polka dance could come from the fabric printing trade: each section of a polka-dot print shows one and a half dots, something like the one and a half musical beats in a polka rhythm. So it is possible that the printed term drifted into a general description of such fabric.

Spanish flamenco dancers often wear dresses covered in spots but they're not called flamenco dots — the Spanish call them *lunares*.

 Is it correct to say that a person is *pontificating* when that person is not a pope?

The *Oxford Concise Dictionary* says that pontificate refers only to the duties of a pope, whereas pontify means acting authoritatively, as if one *were* a pope, and especially if one is being a bit pompous and claiming infallibility.

The Oxford *is* academically correct, but it can be a losing battle when you're up against a huge tide called general usage, which has moved the word pontify into near-oblivion.

So, the Oxford is standing out for accuracy but is beginning to concede that, in the 20th century, the word pontificate has come to mean acting in a pontiff-like manner. Nowadays pontify and pontificate are interchangeable.

So you don't have to be a pope to pontificate — you can be acting as if you were a pope, and expecting everyone to believe that everything you say is immovably correct.

Q **What is a *poodle-faker*?**

A poodle-faker is a man who specialises in being friendly
with women who might be useful for his promotion, either socially
or professionally. He becomes overpolite and attentive, rather like
a lapdog, and is rewarded with friendly affection and either
invitations or recommendations. The expression has been used
quite often in the military, about young officers who cultivate the
goodwill of senior officers' wives. It's a derogatory term, of course:
military men do not commonly have a high opinion of poodles —
or those who fake their behaviour.

Q **Where does the word *poppycock* come from?**

It's an expression that developed in the United States, based
on the Dutch word *Pappekak* which means faeces that are not firm.
The actual origin of the word is Latin, *carcare*, but it was the Dutch
version that became known in the States.

This Dutch word is related to three English words: pap,
meaning soft food especially for babies and invalids; cack, meaning
a kind of childish word for excrement; and poppycock, which is a
combination of them both, meaning worthless material or
nonsense.

Q **Is it true that *posh* means port out starboard home?**

It was published for years that 'port out starboard home'
referred to bookings on steamships travelling to and from India,
when rich people paid extra to ensure the cabins on the cooler
side of the ship both ways. This explanation is now discredited as
a fiction: researchers can find no evidence whatever that port out
starboard home was an expression or a practice ever used.

But there was a word poosh, with two o's, or sometimes spelled
push, which meant smart and dandified. P.G. Wodehouse uses
the word in describing a character with a bright waistcoat which

he says is 'quite the most push thing at Cambridge'. The modern word posh is widely believed to be a variation on that word poosh.

 Where does *prang* come from?

Its exact time and place of origin isn't known, but the word prang was certainly in use in Britain by 1940, mainly as RAF slang for a crash landing or an incident that damaged an aircraft.

It's thought to be more or less onomatopoeic, prang being a made-up word that imitates the effect of metal being impacted.

Q **What is the origin of *prat*?**

Prat is a very old word indeed, so old that its exact origin is unknown, but for 400 years it meant buttocks or bum. The word has gone through an interesting extension, followed by a subsequent shortening.

Since the stock-in-trade of knockabout comedians was to fall over on their bottoms a lot, prat-fall became the description of someone who looked foolish by falling over. Then the term expanded its horizons to include anyone who looked foolish, whether they fell over or not. Eventually the term was shortened again, just to prat, to describe a person who *was* foolish.

But curiously, in some circles, the same short word prat shifted from its original meaning of a unisex bottom to refer specifically to female genitalia. And, in doing so, it became an extremely offensive thing to say about a man.

Q **The use of the word *precinct* somehow seems to suggest American police. Where does it come from?**

There are many words in our language that mean area, whether a political area, a geographic area or an area of interest: province, ward, electorate, riding, catchment, borough. Precinct is simply another one of those — it's a perfectly respectable word that means an area. It comes from the Latin *praecinctum, cinctum* meaning girdled or encircled, and that's the clue, because precinct usually means a defined area.

It's a bit different from electorate or province because precinct can mean either a very firmly defined place, such as part of a cathedral or a section of a city, or it can quite rightly be used in a more vague sense such as saying that 'a murder took place within the precincts of the dance hall', meaning somewhere near the dance hall but not far away.

In the United States the word is used widely to name election districts with a distinct line around them, and also areas of police authority. And although it isn't common in New Zealand, its use by Nelson Town Planning is absolutely legitimate because its heritage precincts are probably defined areas of the city.

 Why are things *in a pretty pass*?

There are 43 meanings of the word pass in English and they nearly all have something to do with allowing things to move from one place to another. But there is a use in which pass means a state of affairs or a condition.

Nobody seems to know who first used the expression pretty pass but it seems to be an example of alliterative irony: it is ironic to use the word pretty about something which is deplorable, and combined with pass it makes an amusing alliteration.

In modern vernacular when something goes wrong people often say, 'That's great', which is the same sort of irony, but without the alliteration.

 Which is the correct way to refer to the *prime minister*? Should it be Right Honourable or The Right Honourable?

There is no rule — a prime minister is accorded the title Right

Honourable but there is no necessity for a 'the'. It is sometimes inserted, especially when speaking about the prime minister, because it may help the verbal balance or flow of a phrase, but the established protocol does not require it — as it does, say, for British royalty where you are required formally to write The Princess Royal or The Princess Anne.

(This difference between speaking and writing often happens. A magazine called *Listener* has been well-known in New Zealand for over 60 years but it is usually spoken of as *the Listener*, although there is no 'the' in the title and never has been. Speaking about the magazine just flows more easily with an inserted 'the'.)

Q   Where does the word *propaganda* come from?

It actually has quite a simple history and we use the verb from it all the time — propagate. It comes from two Latin words for cut and fasten, which together make the word propagate, to reproduce.

In 1622, when Pope Gregory XV was the pontiff, there was a big committee dedicated to creating ways of enlarging the numbers adhering to the Roman Catholic faith, and it was called the Sacre Congregatio de Propaganda Fide, the sacred congregation for propagating the faith — spreading the news around. But of course the idea was very much to promote the faith as desirable, and to influence people to become believers.

So in reality, the word propaganda should mean simply propagating or spreading about, but since that Roman Catholic committee the word has gradually gone into popular usage meaning information whose dissemination is controlled, very organised information that is intended to influence those who hear it.

Q   Why do people say *proven* when they mean *proved*?

Formerly the word proven was used only by the Scottish judiciary as in proven or not proven at the end of a court case.

Now it seems to have become an advertising adjective, as in 'of proven quality'. Is this just another example of our sheep-like tendency to adopt any usage from the United States? No, the word does exist but, strictly, proven is the past participle and should have an auxiliary. Proved is the past tense.

Q **Can some light be shed on the expression *pull your finger out*?**

It means to get going, work efficiently and is believed to have originated in the RAF sometime before the Second World War. Originally the expression was *take* your finger out.

It was always a vulgar phrase but it didn't actually mean what most people thought it meant. Servicemen are reputed to have said it to their fellows whose relationships with women had not yet reached full intimacy — they were advised to cease preliminaries and start concentrating on more satisfying activities.

Originally, the phrase was never said in polite company, though occasionally a Latinate version of the phrase was used when someone would say de-digitate as an admonition. But the original version was wrenched into public fame in October 1961 when Prince Philip said it right out loud in a widely reported speech to a large gathering of businessmen. Advising them that Britain must not become complacent, HRH said, 'Gentleman, it is time that we must pull our finger out.' And a startled world realised that the expression had moved from the locker room to the front pages.

Q **Why do we say *put your best foot forward*?**

Human beings have only two feet, and to have the best of anything you must have three: positive, comparative, superlative — good, better, best. So, speaking literally, we can really only put our better foot forward because we only have two. But the expression now really means do your utmost, extend yourself, try your hardest; it has long ago lost any connection with actual feet.

Q Why do we have a holiday for the *Queen's Birthday* in June?

The custom of celebrating a monarch's birthday was started during the reign of William IV (1830–1837). When his grandson Edward VII came to the throne in 1901 he decided his November birthday was a bad time of year for a holiday (too cold in England) so he moved the actual celebration to England's mid-summer. The following monarch, George V, found this convenient as his birthday was in June.

But his son George VI's birthday was 14 December, so he stuck to the existing custom of an 'official' birthday in June. Elizabeth II has a birthday in April (which can be quite a pleasant time in England) but is believed to have stuck to the June celebration out of deference to Australia and New Zealand celebrating Anzac Day in April and wanting to keep the two occasions separate.

Q Where does the phrase *queer my pitch* come from?

This expression means to spoil the action in someone's field of activity and it dates back over 100 years. It has nothing to do with a cricket pitch. There are 36 different meanings for the word pitch and this one refers to an old-time fairground or market, where the man who was selling his wares or promoting a show by calling out loud was referred to as having a pitch. The pitch was both the area declared to be his, and when he was in action, the sales patter he constantly used.

If something happened to upset the natural flow of his salesmanship — a heckler, a dog-fight, a shower of rain — it was said to have queered his pitch or damaged the effectiveness of his selling.

Sideshow salesmen or barkers are not as familiar now but the expression remains.

 Where in the world would you find a place called *The Quomps*?

There is a place called The Quomps and it's not surprising that it appears in a Thomas Hardy novel because it's near the town of Christchurch in Dorset.

The River Stour flows there, and Quomps is a very old nickname for its banks. The word can still be heard there to describe that part of the bank, and sometimes in summer a rock festival is held on that very place, and it is called Stomping on the Quomps.

Q Why is a prominent gentleman in Fiji spelt *rabuka* but consistently pronounced Ra*m*buka, when there is no m in his name?

There are two stories relevant to this question — one has a logical explanation and the other doesn't.

First, the logical story. It is widely believed that when early European explorers were travelling through the Pacific, they took down the names of places which locals told them and tried to make maps. Now in those days, they had to carry little boxes full of lead letters and mount them in a frame to print. Many Pacific languages have such an abundance of the letters n and m that eventually these cartographers had no more of these left in their boxes, so they simply left them out.

Hence to this very day you'll find maps identifying a place as Pago Pago, without an n, when everyone who's ever lived there or visited there will know that it is actually pronounced Pango Pango, and always has been.

Now, the second story. Many languages contain words that are pronounced quite differently from how they look. English is absolutely full of them. For instance, the word official has ci in the middle, but is pronounced sh. Then you see the word position with ti in the middle and that's also pronounced sh. Other languages do it too. Look at the Polish name, Lech Walesa: you won't see the n sound in the surname but it's necessary to say it.

When the Fijian language is written down, there are a number of invisible consonants that cannot be seen but must be voiced when you speak. So the way some words look is not the way they should actually be said — sometimes there is an invisible m or n or even a th.

For instance, in Fijian the consonant d, when it's spoken, has a slight n inserted before it. Hence the airport spelt Nadi is always pronounced Nandi. Similarly with rugby player Joeli Vidiri.

And the letter b when spoken has a slight m in front of it, so that the b is usually pronounced as the sound in the English word timber. So the gentleman whose name is written as Rabuka must, when being pronounced, have a slight m inserted before the b — Rambuka.

 What is the essential difference between a *raisin* and a *sultana*?

Raisins are larger, normally made from red grapes and often have seeds; sultanas are smaller and usually made from white seedless grapes. However, there is a difference in the origin of the *words*.

What we call sultanas were originally made from a type of grape called the Smyrna grape, which came from Turkey, and was made into a sweetish wine, or dried, and the name of that dried fruit retained a name connected with the area from which they came: sultana is basically an Arabic word that means the wife of a sultan.

In English dried red grapes are called raisins, from the French word *raisin*, which simply means grapes. Usually, French people say *raisin* when they mean grapes, and *raisin sec*, dried grapes, when they mean what we call raisins.

 When the threads are pulled apart in a knitted rayon cord it is described as *ravelled*, but can also be described as *unravelled*. Which is right?

They both are. This is a bizarre case of a word and its own negative both meaning the same thing. Ravel can mean to tangle or tease out and fray, but it can also mean to reduce something knitted or tangled, to separate strands, which is essentially the same as *unravelled*. If you look up ravel in some dictionaries, it gives the meaning unravel, as in the famous example in *Macbeth*: 'Sleep that knits up the ravell'd sleeve of care'.

There are others: flammable means the same as inflammable; cleave means both to stick to and to tear apart; chuffed can mean pleased or displeased.

 Why does the phrase *real estate* contain the word *real*? What does this actually mean?

The word real comes ultimately from the Latin *res*, meaning thing. Thus its various modern meanings are to do with truth, things that exist or occur in the physical world. It often occurs as a qualifier, e.g. referring to value measured in terms of actual price, income and purchasing power, as opposed to nominal value.

Real estate is a term that generally means property which is immovable — it is land, it exists; there's no more of it being made and it can't be carried away. There's another shade of meaning in legal documents such as a will, where you could have a substantial estate, with thousands of dollars of shares and trusts and annuities, but in legal terms those parts of your estate will be described separately from anything solid that can't be carried or transported, such as land, properties. That is described as real.

Q **What is the origin of the term *redneck*?**

The origin is believed to be South African, from the Afrikaans word *rooinek*, which means red-necked and was a disparaging term used by the Boers to describe British troops during the wars in South Africa 100 years ago.

The word drifted to the United States and, pronounced in English, became a put-down description for someone who favoured segregation of Blacks, or for a poor uneducated white farm worker. The term drifted into general British usage round about 1980 and its meaning has extended to cover the uneducated masses.

We frequently hear the word *refugee*. **Does this word have an exact meaning, or is it just anyone who escapes from a war?**

Refugee is a word that operates on two levels. A dictionary will tell you that a refugee is a person who has fled some danger or problem, especially political persecution.

The finite legal definition of a refugee comes from the 1951 United Nations Convention and the 1967 Protocol on Refugees:

A refugee is a person who owing to a well-founded fear of being persecuted for reasons of:

1. race,
2. religion,
3. nationality,
4. membership of a particular social group or
5. political opinion,

is outside the country of his nationality and is unable or, owing to such fear, is unwilling to avail himself of the protection of the country of his nationality.

Even though a person might fit into any one of the five categories mentioned, that person is not automatically classified as a legal refugee. On arrival in a new country he or she must make an application to the immigration officials of that country for recognition as a refugee. Then the applicant goes through a review process, which is entirely a matter for the laws of the country concerned. The United Nations High Commissioner for Refugees recognises that granting asylum is the unfettered right of a sovereign nation.

After going through a legal review successfully, he or she may be classified officially as a refugee and granted political asylum and given the status of a resident alien. A further stage, some time later, would be the granting of full legal residency and then, even later, comes the possibility of citizenship and a passport.

Is there a difference between *reiterate* and *iterate*?

No. In English, using the prefix re- usually indicates doing something again, as in restore, or reinstate. And iterate means to do something or say something a second time, to repeat it, from the Latin *iterum*, meaning simply *again*.

The curious thing is that reiterate means exactly the same: to go over it again. This just shows that the structure of English is sometimes illogical. And the placing of a prefix, which usually alters the meaning of the word in front of which it is placed, sometimes doesn't change it. Active and pro-active belong in this group: they mean the same thing and the prefix is an affectation. The same applies to flammable and inflammable — both mean likely to burn and the prefix is unnecessary.

With iterate and reiterate I can only guess that it's a matter of vocal flow — it's actually easier to say reiterate.

When was the word *relict* in use? It seems to have disappeared.

A relic is something that has survived from the past and relict is an archaic way of spelling it. The word comes from the Latin *reliquiae*, meaning remains.

Both the words relic and remains are still in use but in modern times we generally think of a relic as being something inanimate and the word remains is still occasionally heard to describe a dead human body.

But for quite a long time in the history of English, the word relic or relict was used for both, particularly in parts of the Christian church, where a relic specifically meant a part of the body of a saint or something used or associated with a saint and therefore venerated as having become holy itself, long after the person had died.

Over the history of Christianity, some extraordinary things have been acclaimed as official relics, including the tip of the Devil's tail, a candle lit by Jesus's angel, some hay from the manger in which he was born, some nails used in the crucifixion, the finger of Thomas which had touched Jesus's wounds and a tiny bottle of milk from the Virgin Mary's breast.

Apart from that specialised use of relic, the word also went into common usage in the more general sense of something being left over from someone or something — and this included a man's widow, who was sometimes referred to as a relict of her husband; some widows are described like that on gravestones.

Around about the time when people stopped referring to widows as relicts, the t slowly edged out of the spelling and the word became relic. You will be unlikely to see a modern gravestone describing someone's widow as 'relic of the above'.

 The word *restaurant* has an n in it, but the owner of the restaurant is called a *restaurateur*. Why isn't there an n in *restaurateur*?

The origin of both words is the root of the French verb *restaurer*, to restore. The present participle of that verb, restoring, in French, is *restaurant*. When the word travelled into English, they kept the French participle ending but used it as an English noun — technically it became a gerund (a noun ending in -ing created from a verb). It still made sense: a place you went to for a restoring.

The French way of describing the person who runs the place also follows a French pattern: the root verb *restaur*, plus the affix *ateur*, together making restaurateur.

So in English we are using two French words for two different things and, curiously, they have stayed exactly the same in English as they are in French.

 Why is *rhubarb* the noise made by actors to simulate conversation?

It is a very old theatre tradition, probably dating back to Shakespeare and possibly beyond, that when a crowd onstage is expected to make a general sound there are no actual written words so they all say 'rhubarb' to each other and you just get a sort of vocal confusion — exactly as a large group of people would sound. Nobody really knows why — perhaps it's because the word rhubarb contains the sounds oo and ah, moves the face and is easy to remember.

Over several hundred years this practice of actors has filtered into the language so that, besides the plant, the word rhubarb has taken on an extra area of meaning: noisy nonsense, spoken rubbish, or a noisy argument.

Q What is the origin of *right as rain*?

The phrase, which means everything is correct and as it should be, has been widely used for a century. Writer Nigel Reece says the only explanation is 'the allure of alliteration' — it sounds good. There are other phrases with similar connotations — neat as ninepence, good as gold — and they also have a nice satisfying sound.

Max Beerbohm used this phrase in something he wrote in 1909 but he said 'fit as a fiddle means right as rain', which doesn't help much. Suffice to say that, in many circumstances, rain is a good thing, so the phrase has a certain biological logic.

Q Where does *right down to the wire* come from?

The *Dictionary of American Idiom* says the expression dates from somewhere round 1940. It says the expression means near the finish, taken from American horse-racing where the finishing line of a race is called the wire.

What is the explanation for the strange word *rigmarole*?

In the London Public Records Office there is still a document dating from 1296 and known as the Ragman Roll, which is a register of pledges of loyalty to Edward I, and is prodigiously long, with many alterations and changes of address. The phrase ragman's roll began to carry a sense of some kind of catalogue, especially a very long and convoluted catalogue or list, then eventually it changed slightly to rigmarole, which means a lengthy and unwelcome discourse that is probably boring.

Another possible origin is ragman roll, a list used in a medieval game that described characters in verse.

 Why is the word *roger* used when acknowledging a two-way radio message?

For many years various occupations have used a list of words for clarifying initials — when you make plane reservations, police giving out an instruction, etc. There was even a TV series called *Juliet Bravo*. The system dates from early radio telephony and roger used to be the confirming word for the letter r. At the end of a radio-telephone message, the protocol was to say 'Roger' meaning the letter r which meant received. Roger and out meant that the message had been received and there was no further reply. In later years the alphabet code was changed and nowadays they say Romeo for r.

Of course that was roger as an exclamation or elliptical past participle. When it is used as a present tense verb, to roger, the meaning is quite different, as anyone who's read Robbie Burns will know.

When a person is behaving oddly, why do we say they are *round the bend*?

It is believed to be a mid-19th-century naval term meaning crazy. The origin is not at all clear, but one scholar thinks that it refers to the old term being out of true, where true means correctly aligned, as in a piece of building timber or a fence which is straight. If a thing is out of true, it isn't perfectly straight or perfectly balanced, so it could be said to be round the bend or bent.

 Where does the word *rouseabout* come from?

It has two versions, rouseabout and roustabout, and in New Zealand they both mean the same thing: a handyman-worker on a job, usually rural, who has no defined task — he is terribly busy, but can't be defined as an actual shearer or an actual milker. The word is also often used to describe a general hand in a shearing shed.

The word is believed to derive from an old English word rouseabout which means a rough person who bustles about a lot.

 Is *Rudolph the Red-Nosed Reindeer* a genuine part of the Christmas legend?

No. In 1939 Robert May, who lived in a little Chicago flat with his wife and three children, wrote some Christmas advertising material for a big American shop called Montgomery Ward. By this time, the reindeer Clement Moore had invented in his 1822 poem, 'A Visit from Saint Nicholas', were firmly ensconced in the public mind as the creatures who drew Santa Claus's sleigh — which by now the advertising people had placed in the sky, because that was pretty. Robert May wrote a fanciful poem about another reindeer who didn't fit the sleek mould of Dasher and Dancer and all the others. He was an unglamorous reindeer with a red nose, and his name was Rudolph.

Montgomery Ward printed the poem as a giveaway pamphlet and it was tucked into the parcels of anyone who bought a Christmas gift from one of its many branches: over the following 10 years they actually gave away 10 million copies of the poem, which became sufficiently well known to be the subject of a little movie cartoon.

But it still didn't make Mr May rich, until his brother-in-law Johnny Marks took the poem and set it to music. Then, in 1949, a miracle happened — the cowboy star Gene Autry decided to record the song and that record changed the history of mythology.

The public loves an underdog and Rudolph was exactly that. He was somewhere between the Ugly Duckling and Cinderella and, red-nosed though he was, he did get to go to the ball. The record sold 50 million copies and Rudolph has been with us ever since. The writer, Robert May, died in 1976. By then he had six children and lived in a lovely house.

So Rudolph the Red-Nosed Reindeer doesn't really have a role in the genuine Christian heritage of the Christmas season, but he does have his place in the folklore created by American advertising.

Q **Should we sing Britannia *rule* or *rules* the waves?**

'Rule Britannia' was the hit song from the popular *Alfred: a Masque* written by James Thomson and Thomas Arne and produced in 1740. Thomson was a famous Scottish poet who contributed the words of 'Rule Britannia' to the English language plus a great deal else . . . including the phrase 'elegant sufficiency', which is in his famous poem, 'The Seasons'.

People are inclined to sing 'Britannia rules the waves' but that isn't right. 'Britannia rules the waves' would be a simple statement of naval supremacy, but the song is much bossier than that, it actually says 'Britannia rule the waves' in the imperative. It's a command — Britannia (you go out and) rule the waves.

It is not true that the song originally said Briton rules the waives, meaning to overlook, dismiss or abandon. Waive comes from a 13th-century French word and we find it in modern English when a rule is waived, or in the word waif. It would make sense — Britain wanted to be seen as merciful and forgiving and was big-hearted about waiving rules — but the *Oxford Dictionary of Quotations* certainly gives it as waves in the song.

 People always say they will *run off* some photocopies. Why run off?

The word run has many meanings. And run off has two wide usages in New Zealand.

One of those has always been associated with farming — a run tends to mean an area of farming land that is open rather than fenced. Farmers in New Zealand have used the term run-off for years, meaning a piece of land that is geographically separated from the main farm. Run-off also means the amount of rainfall carried off an area by streams or rivers.

But run off (no hyphen, the verb), meaning to reproduce mechanically, is not a new phrase; it seems to date back to the Industrial Revolution. From about the middle of the 19th century, the term was used to describe a line of goods that were being produced mechanically but probably all looked the same.

It has settled quite logically onto the photocopying process, where everything comes out looking exactly the same, and it is still used in factories where people run off 100 shoes or 1000 salt cellars, all of which are identical. These are often called a run.

 What is a *runcible spoon*?

Nobody knows. Its most famous appearance is in Edward Lear's 'The Owl and the Pussycat'. Some people believe it means a kind of spoon that is divided into three curved prongs but there's little or no evidence that Lear meant that. The general belief is that it's a cute word he simply made up.

S

Who was *St Fiacre*?

St Fiacre became a monk in Kilfiachra (sometimes known as Kilfera) in Ireland but he moved to France, where the bishop said he could have as much land as he could till in one day. Fiacre cleared enough land to set up a monastery where travellers often stayed.

Legend says that he was a marvellous gardener, and admiration abounded for the wonderful vegetables he grew to feed guests who ate at the monastery. That is why he has become the patron saint of gardeners and florists.

But Fiacre was very much against women, who were not allowed into his enclosure, and any who sneaked in suffered severe punishments. The belief that he inflicted great discomfort on women seems to be the reason why he is also listed in the *Wordsworth Dictionary of Saints* as the patron saint of people suffering venereal diseases.

When Fiacre died, in approximately AD 670, many miracles and medical cures were attributed to him and pilgrims travelled to his shrine. Some of the pilgrims who had haemorrhoids believed they would be cured if they sat on the stone Fiacre used to sit on.

The pilgrims left from Paris, at a spot where a famous hotel, Hôtel St Fiacre, was built. And in the mid-17th century this is believed to have been the first place in the world to offer horse-drawn carriages for hire, thus giving the French language the word *fiacre*, and the concept of transport for hire that developed into what we call taxis. St Fiacre, whose feast day is 30 August or 1 September, is also the patron saint of taxi drivers.

Q *Santa Claus* is always mentioned as coming from a cold climate — Finland, Lapland, the North Pole — but does anyone know where he really comes from?

Yes, we do know where Santa Claus comes from. It's an extraordinary example of how literature and commerce can combine almost to obliterate the actual facts, because Santa Claus didn't come from anywhere near the North Pole; he was born and bred in Turkey.

St Nicholas was born in Patara in Turkey and he lived and died in that country. He became a bishop in the town of Myra, and died there, about AD 399. Some of his bones can still be visited in the museum in the city of Anatolya in Turkey, and there is a bronze statue of him nearby, showing him surrounded by children and with a sack on his back. His church is still there, but since it is now about 1500 years old the ground has built up and the main part of the church is 7 metres below the surface.

In those 1500 years, there have been a lot of additions to the image of St Nicholas. Not much is known about him anyway, but a legend developed that he was very kind to poor children, and that he once saved a family of poor girls from being sold into slavery by secretly dropping gold coins down their chimney.

He died on 6 December, which became commemorated in some places around Europe as a time for giving gifts and being unselfish, in his honour. This practice continued for several hundred years, with Nicholas dressed as a bishop, riding a white horse.

When early Dutch settlers went to live in New York, known originally as New Amsterdam, they took the St Nicholas celebrations with them, and paraded in the streets with someone dressed as a bishop. They called him by his Dutch name, *Sinterklaas*, and American journalists, reporting the festivities, spelt this wrongly, so that in 1810 there came one of those wonderful examples of a name being born through a printing mistake: they wrote down Santa Claus.

This was the beginning of the huge change that took place in people's perception of dear old Turkish St Nicholas. New York in December was cold, and the men portraying Nicholas were Dutch, so a vague idea of furs and ruddy faces began to be associated with the name.

The master stroke of transformation took place in 1822 when a poet called Clement Moore wrote a poem about St Nicholas, not Santa Claus, and he created, from his imagination, the jolly personality, the bundle of toys, the white beard, the generous girth *and* the eight reindeer. This poem was titled 'A Visit from Saint Nicholas', but almost everyone in the English-speaking world knows it by the opening line: 'Twas the night before Christmas'. Notice also that it moved the Nicholas celebration date from 6 to 24 December.

This poem more or less crystallised the image of Santa Claus as he is known today. In the public's mind, the name of St Nicholas in the poem somehow became transposed to the new words they'd heard, Santa Claus.

There were two other major developments. Clement Moore's poem depicted St Nicholas as a cheerful little elf, but when people started to dress up as him, naturally he gradually grew to normal size. And of course the first drawings of this new legend, in 1863, were published only in black and white so the colour of what he wore wasn't too important. In fact 19th-century Santa Clauses often wore brownish or greenish costumes.

But by 1870, the fairly newly invented figure of Santa Claus was firmly entrenched in the American idea of selling. The legend was encouraged that everyone must receive gifts at Christmas, so of course everyone must *buy* them. Santa became part of big business. And then came the final stroke — the invention of colour printing.

Green and brown don't look as striking in colour as does red. So the reddish bishop's robes which the early Dutchmen had worn when celebrating St Nicholas were brought back into the black and white furs shown in early illustrations of Santa and Santa Claus erupted into advertising, wearing bright red, mainly because it caught people's attention and sold things better.

American advertising firmly advanced the image of Santa Claus, and almost wiped out his true origins — except in Turkey, of course.

The new Santa Claus practically obliterated the much earlier image of a figure called Father Christmas, who'd been busy since the 15th century. He was connected to the European legend of Woden, the gift-giving god figure, and was usually big and brawny with a hairy chest.

It's almost as if we're talking about two entirely different people: the Turkish St Nicholas who didn't even know where the North Pole was, and the American-invented Santa Claus who dates back only to 1822 and has become an image of marketing, with a cumulatively invented imaginary lifestyle that includes a home in a terribly cold country.

 'Those who cannot remember the past are condemned to repeat it' is attributed to *Santayana*. Who was Santayana?

George Santayana was born in Spain in 1863 but went to study at Harvard University where he eventually became a lecturer in philosophy. He was a respected philosopher, a poet and novelist, a critic and social commentator.

One of his famous books was *The Life of Reason*, published in 1905, and that was where the famous line appeared. He died in 1952.

Q Why are *sausages* called *snags* or *snarlers* or *bangers*?

Snags is an old English dialect word for a small morsel of food. Lancashire has a version of the word in snackies, meaning what we would call nibbles. It could possibly also be related to the word snack, a small amount of food, which itself comes from a Dutch word snakken, meaning bite. In New Zealand we say snacks for small amounts of food, but the word snags seems to have attached itself only to sausages.

Snarler was first published in 1941 as originally Australasian military slang during the Second World War, when servicemen said rather uncharitably that the sausages they were served were probably made from cats and dogs. And they had so much fat that, when cooked, they hissed and spat, or snarled, and really unpleasant ones were also called growlers or barkers, although the last two terms have not gone into common usage.

The British military equivalent of the Australasian snarlers was the word bangers, again because of the noise sausages often make when they're frying. British servicemen described this as a bang, and Australasians called it a snarl. Hence, bangers and snarlers.

Q Why do people say they feel *seedy*?

It's quite straightforward: a verbal contraction of the expression going to seed. It is generally perceived that garden plants look their best when they are in flower, but if they move onwards to the state of producing seeds, they tend to look a bit straggly and not quite so glamorous. Sometimes you are encouraged not to let plants go to seed if you want a garden to remain looking good. Hence, if a person is looking untidy and not as fit as they used to be, you'll hear someone say they're going to seed. From that has evolved the expression seedy, meaning not quite crisp and flourishing.

The difference is that, when said about a person, going to seed is quite often a long and even permanent process, but when someone says it about themselves, that they are feeling seedy, the straggly state is usually temporary.

Q Why do we talk about *setting the world on fire*?

Shakespeare doesn't have it exactly — he has 'Then may I set the world on wheels' in *Two Gentlemen of Verona* (1594) — and Chaucer has 'Set the world at six and seven' (1374).

But in 1940 American writers Eddie Seiler and Sol Marcus and composer Bennie Benjamin wrote a song called 'I Don't Want to Set the World on Fire'. It was first recorded by a group called

184

The Rockets, and didn't make much of an impact. But in 1941, the Mills Brothers and the Ink Spots took the song up, sung much more slowly, and it became not only a hit but a standard.

That song is so recognisable that I suggest that the phrase about setting the world on fire may well have been originally written by Eddie Seiler and Sol Marcus. (It sometimes happens that a song puts an expression into the language, e.g. grandfather clock.)

When a person fancies someone, why are they described as *setting their cap* at them?

In centuries past, people wore hats a great deal more than they do now. There were special hats men put on when they were smoking, distinct hats women wore if they were widows, elaborate bonnets for going visiting in, caps for wearing around the house, even long floppy hats people wore to bed.

Young women often wore lightweight hats or caps made of muslin, especially if there were visitors coming to the house. The expression grew out of the belief that if the household was expecting a visit from an attractive young man, the daughters of the family would take particular care over their muslin headgear, making sure it was fresh and clean and crisp. Less reverent members of the family, probably their brothers, would say the girls were setting their cap at the visitor.

Gradually, when people stopped wearing hats all the time, the expression began to mean the way you were behaving — organising yourself so that you came to the attention of someone you fancied.

Shambolic — where does this come from?

It comes from shambles, which is a modern version of an old Latin word for a bench or table; in English it came to mean the table used by butchers for chopping beasts up into portions. So a floppy disorganised walk was called a shamble because the legs were all over the place like legs lying on a butcher's table, and shambles became the word for a slaughterhouse or a place where meat was prepared. A famous part of York is still called The Shambles, from the time when butchers' shops were centred there. And because meat preparation is always messy, the word shambles came to mean disorder.

But it remained a noun, a shambles, until some bright spark turned it into an adjective and said, 'This is a shambolic state of affairs.' Behold, a new word was born.

 Q Since ships have no gender, why are they always referred to as *she*?

This dates way back to when sea-going vessels were always dedicated to a goddess, whose protection they were thought to be under, and whose effigy was affixed to the prow. As belief in goddesses diminished, the female figure in the prow was retained as a decoration, but the habit had grown of referring to the ship and the goddess as one and the same — thus, she.

Later in history, by extension, the habit of using she for vehicles that moved became fairly commonplace — even without goddesses being involved.

Q Where does the expression *she'll be right* come from?

It's a combination of Australian and New Zealand usage. The Australian vernacular often uses she to mean it, e.g. she'll be Jake. Taking this Australian habit and adding will be right arose in Australia in the 1940s and the phrase is now used in both countries.

Why is the word *sheila* sometimes used of women in New Zealand?

Sheila is a term of disapprobation that has been taken over and used by its subjects, who now use it with some pride and humour. This sometimes happens. The BBC explains the term Desert Rats as an equivalent development — Mussolini said it about the troops as an insult, but the troops took it up themselves as a gesture of defiance, and eventually of great pride.

Sheila is an Irish name, derived from Celtic, and which has also been used as a slang term in the British Isles since 1832; it surfaced in New Zealand at the end of the 19th century. Originally it was a shade disrespectful — a young woman to whom one was not married — but eventually love took over and sheila was no longer appropriate, until marriage actually happened, upon which she became The Old Sheila.

New Zealand women seem to realise, very sensibly, that if you can't beat it, join it, and sheila has moved in to be the opposite of bloke — a user-friendly gender description. Writer Sandra Coney explains that the term now means gutsy woman; the word is no longer a put-down but a cheerful and self-confident acknowledgement that women can do their own thing in a room of their own which they can call, without a blush, the sheila's shed.

 If cows are always in a herd, and sheep are always in a flock, why is the person who looks after the sheep always described as a *shepherd*, a herder of sheep?

The word *herd* comes from an old Greek word meaning a group, and in English it has come to refer to a large group of animals, usually mammals, and usually cows, goats or pigs, but it used to include sheep.

One of the archaic uses of the word herd was to describe a person who looked after *any* form of livestock at all. This has remained with us, in shepherd and goatherd, even though the sheep in question are now commonly called a flock, which comes from the Latin for downy, fluffy things. (We still use that word for mattress fillings and wallpaper that has been made fuzzy.) So the word for a group of sheep changed but the word for the person looking after them didn't.

Q **What does the word *shickered* mean?**

There is one school of thought that the word, which has various spellings, and means drunk, is from an Arabic source, and was brought into English by soldiers. But there is a Hebrew word, *shikor*, very old indeed, which was adapted into the Yiddish language spoken by Jewish people in Europe. When many Yiddish-speaking Jews went to live in New York about 1900, the word *shikker*, meaning drunk, was introduced to English-speaking people. And you still occasionally hear the word in the United States. It became particularly popular in Australia and New Zealand.

Q **Why is a petticoat called a *shimmy*?**

Chemise is a French word, and shimmy is an Anglicised way of saying that, but they both come from an old Latin word, *camisia*, which itself was borrowed by the Romans from an Arabic word, *quamis*. Both words described a loose garment falling from the shoulders. By the time it entered Old French it still meant a loose garment falling from the shoulder, but in general worn underneath other clothing. Nearly 1000 years ago the French word chemise drifted into English and it's been spelt several different ways over ten centuries, but the meaning has remained similar.

Along with the popularity of the term shimmy there came a new dance that was characterised by a lot of shaking and sliding, rather like a garment not fitted to the body, and hence it was called the shimmy.

Curiously, the old Latin word *camisia* also survived in English in a rather more recognisable form. Parallel with the taking-over of the French word chemise, the English also developed the word camisole, which is much more directly from the Latin. But whereas a chemise or shimmy is usually a petticoat, slip or underdress with very little shaping, a camisole is an upper-body garment with some sort of shape and possibly shoulder straps.

 Queen Victoria's diary tells that when she and Prince Albert first went to live at Balmoral Castle, an old *shoe* was thrown after them into the house, for luck. Why?

Social researcher Rudolph Brasch explains that through the ages shoes have carried a great deal of symbolism: they have been seen as aids to fertility, and as the home of the soul. When people were beginning a journey it was a custom to throw an old shoe at them — it was believed to convey to the travellers all the good luck and experience of the shoe's former owner. Old shoes carried more use and wisdom than new — and of course new shoes have always been expensive, so using old shoes had an economic influence as well.

Shoes also carry a connotation of ownership, dating as far back as the Bible — in Psalm 60 'Over Edom itself I cast my shoe' — meaning rulership and domination.

At weddings, old shoes symbolise future fertility, they convey good luck to the married couple and they signify the bride's family transferring ownership of or control over her to her new married state.

In 1855 when that diary entry of Queen Victoria's was written, she and Albert had been married for nearly 15 years but the throwing of shoes still carried powerful signals of good luck, wisdom and, of course, their dominion over Balmoral Castle, which was new at the time.

The cultural significance of feet and shoes remains strong. We talk about being under the boot of tyranny; by law royals may not be depicted on a mat; some religions prefer shoes to be left outside a place of worship; Maori are cautious about things associated with feet and when people are formally welcomed in Maori, they thank the hosts for giving a place for their feet — a turangawaewae.

Q **Where does the word *shonky* come from?**

Shonky is claimed by the *Oxford Dictionary* as being an Australian word, which came into common use late in the 20th century, meaning unreliable.

Perhaps it is related to the British word wonky, which is truly ancient, and derives from an English dialect word *wancol*, meaning unstable and liable to break.

Q **What does it mean to say *show you round the kitchen*?**

This is a way of saying that if you don't do so-and-so then you're about to get some sort of punishment — probably a good thrashing. It's believed to have originated in Ulster in Northern Ireland.

It is thought that the expression came about because many houses had a combined kitchen and what we would call a living room, so the kitchen may have been quite big. A parent who was about to take a strap or a branch to a naughty child was inclined not to stand in one place but to move around so they could get a good swing.

Q **Why do people say *shuffle off this mortal coil*?**

It means to die, and it's a direct quote from Shakespeare's *Hamlet*, the famous 'To be or, not to be' speech, in which Hamlet says, 'For in that sleep of death, what dreams may come, / When we have shuffled off this mortal coil.' And he was using the word coil in its 16th-century meaning of the trouble and activities of the world.

Did *Siegfried Sassoon* pack his *Oxford Dictionary* when he moved house in 1914?

His biographer said he did, but this was queried because the dictionary wasn't published until 1928. But it has been pointed out that although the dictionary was *completed* in 1928, its early sections started coming out in 1884 so it was quite possible that Sassoon possessed some of those early sections in 1914.

 Is it true that '*Silent Night*' was an accident?

Yes, it was an accident. The little church in the Austrian village of Oberndorf was getting ready for Christmas in 1818, and someone discovered that mice had eaten holes in crucial parts of the church organ.

The priest, Franz Grüber, and the organist, Joseph Mohr, very hastily made up a special Christmas song that could be accompanied by just one guitar — which was fairly revolutionary in 1818. They performed the song at the Christmas service that year, and it might have been totally forgotten except that the man who came to repair the mouse holes in the organ took a copy of the song back to the city of Leipzig. He handed the song — 'Stille Nacht' — on to other people. It was sung in Leipzig, and soon became one of the most famous Christmas songs in the world. The village of Oberndorf is still there of course, and the church displays the original music of 'Silent Night', and the guitar on which it was played.

Why is *silver beet* called silver when it is actually green?

Silver beet is known by at least two other names — Swiss chard and spinach beet. It's been called silver beet in New Zealand since the start of the 20th century (it appeared in print in 1902) and this could be because it *isn't* all green — it has very wide prominent stems of silvery-white, often almost as wide as the green leafy bit, and this isn't at all like the similar plant, which we call spinach.

 What are the origins of three words used in mathematics: *sine, cosine* and *tan*?

Some of the traditions and words of modern mathematics stem from ancient Greece and some words are related to Hindu and Arabic words, which were then translated back into Latin.

Sine comes from the Latin *sinus*, meaning a bend. Sinus is still found in English in words like sinuous (moving in curves like a snake does) or sinus (a curved cavity within the body). In mathematics, the Latin word eventually became sine, sometimes shortened to sin. It concerns calculations involving the radii or circles but also relates to measurements in trigonometry. The word isn't always associated with curves but that's how it came into use.

Cosine simply adds co- to the word sine. Co- is a reduced form of the Latin *com* and indicates the meaning of jointly, mutually, in equality. So adding co- to sine often refers to the complementarity of an angle.

Tan, a word often seen in maths, is an abbreviation of tangent, which is also from a Latin word, *tangere*, meaning to touch. You'll find it in other English words like tangible — something physical rather than something imagined. In mathematics, a tangent is usually a line that touches something else but doesn't intersect it. One thing touches another, hence tangent.

 The word *singlet* is curious. Where does it come from?

For several hundred years, men wore a fairly tight top, with sleeves and a little skirt. These varied a great deal, with padding and decoration, but they were firm in construction, and because they always had an outer layer of fabric and an inner layer, a lining, they were called doublets, meaning two-layered.

The lining was important. It not only kept the garment firm, but the outer layer often had slashes cut in it so that the brightly coloured lining showed, or the lining was pulled through the slash and puffed out a bit. Rich people, including Henry VIII, had slashed doublets with jewels and embroidery in the bits of lining that poked through.

But during the 18th century fabrics and lifestyles changed, and some garments for men's torsos were made with only one layer of fabric. These floppier tops came to be worn underneath rather than on top, and usually had no sleeves, and — the important bit — no lining. So because the traditional top had two layers of fabric and was called a doublet, the undergarment with only one layer of cloth was called a singlet.

Ordinary singlets have no sleeves, but you can get a singlet with sleeves in it, and these were originally contrived by an ancestor of Princess Diana's who was feeling the cold. Her maiden name was Spencer, and to this day the sleeved singlets are called spencers.

 Where does the phrase *sitting up like Jackie* come from?

It's an Australian expression dating to approximately 1930. Jackie was a slang term for an Aboriginal, and somehow the expression grew that sitting up like Jacky means sitting straight and being well behaved.

 What is the origin of the expression *at sixes and sevens*?

It means a confusion of things, or people who are in disagreement, and could well be several thousand years old. It comes from the Book of Job in the Bible, so it could originally have been ancient Hebrew, but the authorship of the Book of Job is not clear and some scholars think its structure represents a style from outside Israel, possibly Egyptian. So the truthful answer is that nobody knows what language the phrase originally comes from, but we do know what the original says.

Translated into English, the phrase says 'God shall deliver thee in six troubles, yea in seven' and that is interpreted to mean that there will be no particular order and no particular number — the troubles are not going to be in organised, pre-ordained circumstances. Hence, everything will be at sixes and sevens.

 Old record players have a little sign on them saying 16 rpm. What does this mean?

It means 16 revolutions per minute. After wax cylinders, recordings went flat and played at 78 revolutions per minute. Things stayed that way for about 30 years, until about 1950 when the new long playing records became sensationally available. They were the same size as the old 78s but made of more flexible material so they would not break, and they played at 33 rpm so much more material could be fitted on them.

Soon after that, in the mid-1950s, someone invented records which could be played at 45 rpm, slightly faster than 33 rpm, but they were smaller, so usually only a single song fitted on them. And, about the same time, it was planned to produce records that played at 16 rpm, half the speed of the popular 33 rpm. These would have had nearly an hour of material on them before you had to turn them over.

The appliance industry got onto this very quickly, and immediately started producing gramophones that could play at 78, 45, 33 or 16 rpm. But something wasn't quite right. When records that played at 16 rpm were actually made, it was discovered that they were so slow that their music reproduction wasn't very good; they were really only suitable for the spoken word, like a sort of talking book. And quite soon 16 rpm records disappeared over the horizon.

Most electric gramophones were made with a selector that could play records at 78, 45, or 33. One that has 16 rpm as well would be quite a rare artefact, a record even rarer.

Is *skite* a New Zealand word?

No, it's from a British word and the full original term is blatherskite. Blather comes from an Old Norse word *blathra*, meaning nonsense, and skite seems to be interchangeable with skate in some dialects of northern England and Scotland to mean a talkative silly person.

So a blatherskite was a noisy person who talked a lot of nonsense. In recent years, Australians and New Zealanders have shortened the word to just skite, and slightly changed its application so that it means irritating people by boasting unnecessarily.

 What is the origin of *skulduggery*?

The *Pocket Scots Dictionary* defines *skulduddery* or *sculdudrie* (note the d) as a Scottish term meaning 'unpermitted sex' or 'obscenities and indecencies'. Skulduggery comes from this, but has extended its meaning to include anything underhand.

What is the background to the expression *open slather*?

The actual word slather has a mysterious origin, though it may have originated in the Irish word *slighe*, which means an access or a way.

The word slather is used in three different ways:

(1) Sometimes in Britain nowadays it is used to mean a scolding or even a beating-up: 'The boy received a severe slathering'.

(2) The same word is used in the United States and although it probably has the same ancestry, its meaning there is different. Slather means a large amount, or to spread thickly: 'He slathered butter on his bread'.

(3) The form open slather has only been around since the 19th century, and it's commonly used in Australia and New

Zealand to mean free for all, anything goes. The origin of the expression is not entirely clear, but it's thought to have originated in Australia, and it does have a slim connection with the old Irish word *slighe*, meaning access. So open slather means access from a wide variety of positions — anything goes.

Q **Where does *sleaze* come from?**

Sleaze is a wonderful word, almost onomatopoeic; it sounds like slime and slippery and ooze, and that's more or less what it means — squalid. There is no clear explanation of where the modern usage came from, but references such as *Chambers* and *Oxford* tell us that the word was being used 300 years ago to describe thin, insubstantial fabric. We don't know why sleaze and sleazy nowadays mean squalid and distasteful, but there is probably a connection with the fact that sleaze used to mean fabric that was cheap and nasty.

Q **What does *doing a slinter* mean?**

The expression comes originally from Dutch, then Afrikaans — *schlenter*, then *slenter* — and was adopted from South African slang into New Zealand. It means the same thing here: an underhand trick, a sham, a fast one. It was first seen in print in New Zealand in 1864, with a slightly different spelling.

Q **What is the origin of the word *snob*?**

The word snob originated from the Latin phrase *sine nobilitate* which had been used for years to designate someone who was not of aristocratic birth. This is said to have been written on the guest lists when Roman emperors asked people to a banquet, so the rulers knew who was important and who wasn't. It is also believed to have been written next to the names of students in ancient universities who were not from aristocratic families. Often it was abbreviated to just s.nob.

Unfortunately, the people who were *not* noble, finding themselves surrounded by people who were, tended to try to become like the aristocracy, and because they were in an upper circle by virtue of circumstance, they tended to have an exaggerated disapproval of people who were not part of the upper circle (unlike genuine aristocrats who are normally quite relaxed and comfortable anywhere).

So the abbreviated s.nob began to be associated with people who were unpleasantly conscious of their position, and rather too keen to let other people know about their importance, whether this was deserved or not. Hence the modern word snob and its meaning — one who believes that his or her own position in life justifies being unpleasant to those thought to be lower, and who has an energetic intention to remain on terms with those thought to be higher.

Q   *Snork* — what is the source of that word?

It is regarded as a casual term for a baby, any baby, but only in Australasia. Its exact origin is not entirely clear but language scholars like Eric Partridge believe that it is derived from the word stork — part of the old legend adults told children: that babies were brought by a stork.

This is an ancient story originating in Scandinavia and popularised by Hans Christian Andersen. In some of the Scandinavian areas, storks customarily nest on the chimney-tops of houses. The birds are monogamous, and may live for 70 years, returning to the same chimney every year. Thus the families who live below have ample chance to become familiar with the breeding of storks and the considerate way in which the young treat their ageing parents. Plus, they're sitting on the roof of the house. So an explanation grew that storks could very conveniently drop a new little baby down the chimney.

This explanation is so deeply entrenched in European cultures, including New Zealand, that even today people who've just had a baby are sent greeting cards with a picture of a stork on them, by people who have never seen a stork!

Australians and New Zealanders were party to these legends, but somehow wanted to make the whole issue a bit more pragmatic and less fanciful. (Besides, there are no storks in these countries, to send the babies down the chimneys.) So eventually instead of saying that someone had a visit from the stork, the word stork was corrupted and saying that someone had a snork became an antipodean way of referring to the old legend but putting a vernacular spin on it.

Another possible derivation of snork is an old dialect word in England: *snorken* is a verb used to describe animals grunting. From that the noun snork was used to describe a baby pig, especially in northern England and Scotland, from where the word drifted to Australia and became a noun and was applied to babies.

Q Where does the word *soccer* come from?

The word football is a generic term — games in which a ball is played with the feet. There are at least five kinds. The word evokes different things in Britain, New Zealand, the United States and Australia.

The correct and original name for soccer is Association Football and if you take the three letters s-o-c out of the word association, then add er to them, that is the origin of the word soccer. It's a slang abbreviation. The word soccer has been in use since the late 19th century, and for a short time it was spelt socker but the spelling has simplified. Just don't use the word at all in Britain — they don't like it: it's football to them.

198

Q What is the origin of the phrase *sold down the river*?

It's American, dating from the time when slaves were bought and sold. Plantations on the lower reaches of the Mississippi River were believed to be much harsher than elsewhere, so to be sold down the river was to be betrayed into a bad scene.

Q *Solomon Grundy* was born on Monday. Who was he?

He never existed — the word comes from an Old French word *salmagundy*, which was cold chopped meat mixed with eggs and onions — a sort of hotch-potch or hodge-podge. (In contemporary French the equivalent is *hochepot* or *salmigondis*.) From there it drifted into English in the 18th century meaning a cook, and later because it sounded like a name, Solomon Grundy, people thought it might have been a real person. But it wasn't.

Note, it is not connected with the New Zealand slang grundies meaning men's underpants — a kind of rhyme for undies (which was considered a feminine word).

 How did the *Solomon Islands* get their name? Is it anything to do with being solemn?

No, the Solomon Islands have nothing to do with being solemn. The natives who lived there for centuries were disturbed in 1567 by an explorer from Spain, Alvaro de Mendaña de Neyra. And in the paternalistic vocabulary of the time, he was credited with having 'discovered' the islands — though of course there had been people living there for years. To Mr de Neyra's eyes the inhabitants seemed to be wearing ornaments made from something that looked like gold. And, in a fit of fancy, he imagined he'd found the legendary country mentioned in the Bible's Book of Kings, the land of Ophir from which gold was brought to King Solomon. So, de Neyra announced to the rest of the world that he had named the islands the Solomons.

It is believed to be the only country in the world named after a biblical character — not just mentioned *in* the Bible, like Israel, but named after a biblical person. Countries named after a person are rare: Saudi Arabia is a rare example of a country named after a family and America takes its name from a man's first name. Liechtenstein and Luxembourg are named for their rulers but that might not be their surname; titled people often have surnames quite different from their title — the Princes of Monaco, for instance, have the surname Grimaldi.

 Q **Is there an equivalent for a woman demeaning a man by calling him *sonny*?**

Yes . . . it is demeaning for a man to address a woman as *girlie*.

Q **Why do we call someone a *sook*?**

Sook and sooky are believed to derive from a 10th-century Old English verb *sucan*, which meant to suck. That became a dialect word for a baby, and it might have been influenced by the Welsh word *sweard*, to tame. So sook, or sooky, used to mean just a genuine baby but now has become derogatory and means either someone who acts like a baby, or maybe is a coward.

Q **Where does the expression *sound bite* come from?**

The expression, meaning a short, pithy piece extracted from an interview or speech, began to be used in the 1980s. The practice probably arises from the assumption that the modern public will not follow anything for more than a few seconds, and the use of sound bites has now led to people deliberately making short statements for quick use — 'Give us enough for a sound bite'.

It's called a sound bite because it is a short, quick snap, like a bite. It's apparently unrelated to computer byte but has the undertone of a high-tech approach. Interestingly, it's now used when speaking about television, which has pictures along with the sound bite.

 ### Where does the term *southpaw*, meaning left-handed, originate?

It's American, very American, because it originates in baseball. In regulation baseball, the batter faces east so that the afternoon sun doesn't shine in his eyes. The pitcher is therefore facing west. In the case of a left-handed pitcher, his throwing arm and hand are on the south side of his body, hence the expression southpaw.

Baseball dates way back. Jane Austen mentions it, as do other English writers in the 18th century. It began to interest the Americans in the early 19th century and the first regulations concerning baseball were drawn up in 1845. Formal rules were established in 1920, and the word southpaw has been used among Americans for that long or longer.

 ### How did the expression *sow your wild oats* come about?

This is agricultural vernacular. Wild doesn't actually mean barbaric or violent, but uncultivated, growing in its original raw state — such as wild flowers, wild onions, etc.

Thus, if you plant good cultivated seed, you get reliably good plants, but if you collect seeds in the wild, they may grow into plants that are a bit rough and don't make good produce. A wise farmer will sow good quality cultivated oats; sowing wild oat seed would be foolish, because this would probably give rise to a bad crop.

So sowing wild oats refers to the fact that youthful excessive behaviour doesn't necessarily lead into good, solid adulthood. The expression has been in use since the 16th century with this meaning but nowadays the expression has taken on a distinctly temporary feel: if you sow wild oats when you're young, you probably do get the roughness out of your system, and later on you turn into a good, productive, cultivated oat.

 Why are outspoken people said to call a *spade a spade*, and what does the word *spade* have to do with foreigners or immigrants?

To call a spade a spade is an expression from ancient Greek (*spathë* in Greek meant a flat sword or blade) and originally meant much what it means now — that an honest person would call a spade simply what it was. The expression filtered through into English and has been in this language for over 450 years.

It has gradually taken on a connotation of describing a person who uses outspoken language, quite the opposite of spin doctors and political press secretaries and the people who coined the title crown health enterprise. (That is *not* calling a spade a spade.)

Charles Dickens used the expression in 1854 in the way we use it now: in *Hard Times*, a character says, 'There's no imaginative sentimental humbug about me. I call a spade a spade.'

There's a famous double-ended use of the expression in Oscar Wilde's *The Importance of Being Earnest* when one society bitch says to another 'When I see a spade I call it a spade.' The other society bitch replies, 'I am glad to say that I have never seen a spade. It is obvious that our social spheres have been widely different.'

Spade as a derogatory term for Black Americans is thought to derive from the fact that the symbol for spades on playing cards is always black.

 Why is a thin person sometimes described as *spare*?

Spare comes originally from an Old German word *sparon* and by the time it migrated into English it was *sparian* and then it slowly narrowed down to just spare. Over the years it has gathered no less than 17 slightly different meanings. Certainly the word was once quite commonly used to describe someone who had no excess flesh, and you still occasionally hear it.

There is reputed to have been a tricky incident involving the most famous King of Siam (Mongkut) who was described by a British journalist as *a spare man* because he was thin. The king read this, and was very querulous because he thought it meant he was an unnecessary man, surplus to requirements and used only in emergencies. He didn't know all the 17 meanings.

Spare is one of those irritating words which means the opposite of itself: a spare person is lean without unnecessary weight, but spare can also mean extra, in excess of what is needed.

 Is it possible to be *spic* without being *span*, or must the two always go together?

They've been together for over 400 years so I don't think there's much chance of separating them now; people like emphasising things.

The old meaning of spic is related to the modern word spike. A spic was a shiny new nail. The old meaning of span was a chip, as in a chip of wood. So when people said something was spic and span new they meant it was as if the nails were all gleaming and the wood was freshly shaped.

The expression must have been around during the 1500s — you'll find it in Sir Thomas North's translation of Plutarch's *Lives*, published in 1759: 'gilt armours and purple cassocks, spicke and span new'. In time the expression dropped the word 'new' so that nowadays when you say something is spic and span it doesn't necessarily have to be new, just tidied up and looking good.

(Spick with a k (also spik and sometimes spic) is a derogatory term for foreigners, based on the phrase 'No spika-da-English'.)

When did the term *spin doctor* come into the language?

It came into the language in the 1980s and its first known appearance in print was 1984, when a report on a debate between Ronald Reagan and Walter Mondale mentioned that the statements each was making must have been put together by spin doctors.

The term comes from sports where a skilful thrower can add a spin to the ball which can deceive everyone about the exact path the ball will follow. The expression came to be used in describing people who can arrange words to give a desired impression, rather than making a simple statement of fact.

 Why do we use the term *spitting image*, meaning an exact likeness?

The expression dates back over 100 years in the English language. The word spit has five different meanings in English, and among these is an old one meaning copy. It's related to another meaning — to eject suddenly from the mouth — because, in earlier centuries, when people said something was a spit-and-image of something else, they meant that the resemblance was so close it looked if the copy had been spat out of the mouth of the original. That was the early form of the expression, spit-and-image, a lovely example of grammatical redundancy, since in that context spit and image mean the same thing.

By 1895 and had been dropped from the phrase, and it became spit'n image. After that, the noun became a present participle adjective, and edged into spitting image, which is how we use it now, but still meaning exactly the same as it always has meant: an exact copy.

Alternatively, a historical botanist explains that an ancient form of receipt was to carve notches on a stick, then split the stick into halves, for each party of the transaction to keep. To prove that one had a genuine receipt, the split wooden bits must tally exactly with the other half: to make a splitten image. That survives, by contraction, in spitting image.

Q Why are some things described as *spot on*?

Around the end of the 19th century, a phrase crept into publication, meaning alert, accurate and ready. That phrase was on the spot. Nobody will stick their neck out about whether the much newer phrase spot on is in fact the same, having undergone our old friend The Reversal, but I'm inclined to think this is the case, that spot on is really on the spot back to front. The meaning hasn't reversed, but the words have.

Q Why are potatoes called *spuds*?

The word *spud* has been in use for over 100 years, it's believed to have arisen in Scotland, where it meant potato. Spud is thought to have descended from a word that was quite common 500 years ago: *spudde* or *spudder*. This was a kind of knife, and the word eventually widened its application to mean a small spade, and that's the clue.

Things which were dug up with a spudder were called spuds, and because potatoes were among the things most commonly dug up, the meaning narrowed down so that spuds eventually meant just potatoes.

Q Why do we say *stiff* or *hard cheese*?

It means you're having bad luck and is actually self-explanatory because the word stiff is often used to describe working parts that aren't moving freely. And although cheese shouldn't actually move, neither should it be tough and unyielding. So cheese that is either stiff or hard isn't good enough, and you are unlucky to have been served it.

There are two developments to the expression. In Australia the cheese bit is often left off, and if you have a misfortune someone is likely to say, 'Gee that's stiff' (which is shorthand for stiff cheese). And in New Zealand the expression is occasionally modified into stiff kumara which, I suppose, would be as unwelcome as stiff cheese.

 Is *stove* a peculiarly New Zealand word?

Stove is definitely not a uniquely New Zealand word. Stove is related to the Dutch word *Stoof* and the German *Stufe*, which originally meant a hot room where people sat and sweated. Gradually this came to mean an enclosed space that was heated and then it came to mean an appliance characterised by having an enclosed heated space. In Britain, though, they call a stove a cooker.

What is the origin of saying *stump up*, when offering or lending money to someone?

Two lovely expressions come from tree stumps, both of them American. The stump of a tree used to stand on for meetings etc. has now become political — *to stump*. To stump up has a slightly different meaning and there are two explanations.

To stump a tree meant to pull it out entirely by the roots, leaving nothing. By the 19th century the expression to stump up had arisen, meaning that you had absolutely nothing left; your roots had been pulled out, and you needed money from someone else. Gradually, the expression seems to have transferred to the person giving the money, so that to stump up someone or something means you are backing it financially.

There is also another explanation. To stump up means you hand money over, as if slapping it down onto a flat surface, e.g. a tree stump.

Q What is the origin of *not suffering fools gladly*?

The originating phrase that undoubtedly inspired this comes from the Bible, Corinthians II, Chapter 11, where you'll find the line 'For ye suffer fools gladly, seeing ye yourselves are wise'. It's fairly likely that over the years some assertive souls have pointed out that they do not wish to be included in that, and therefore have said, 'I do *not* suffer fools gladly.' They have dared to turn the Bible back to front!

Q How did the expression *sugar daddy* originate?

It originated in the United States, about 70 years ago and meant then what it means now: an oldish man who spends lavishly on a younger woman, in return for sexual favours. There's no clear explanation about who or why the expression evolved — it just did, and seems to fit the situation perfectly. A saccharin daddy is a sugar daddy without the sex.

Q When is *the sun over the yard arm*?

This one goes back to the times of sailing ships. The yard is a long spar that supports and spreads the sails and the yard arm is one of those, tapered at the ends. An old naval expression had it that when the sun could be seen over the yard arm it was time for a drink.

Nowadays when people say this it has a connotation that the day is slowing down and evening is coming, but in fact it appears that in olden times the opposite was true — that when the sun could be seen over the yard arm it was rising. In some parts of the world, the sun would get to be higher than the yard arm round about noon.

Q **What does the word *suss* mean, as in 'we are sussing out something'?**

It's a trendy abbreviation of suspect or suspicion and is very recent — mid-20th century. Over the last few years suss has broadened its meaning a little. Besides meaning to suspect, to sniff out or discover the truth it now includes the meaning to surmise, to imagine what is likely.

It is very similar to another trendy modern word, recce, which is an abbreviation of reconnoitre, to have a good look at the territory.

 Q **What does the term *swansong* really mean, and is there a definitive answer to where the term comes from?**

The swan figures in many, many legendary images. The Greek god Apollo was believed to have been changed into a swan and this gave rise to a centuries-long belief that, after death, the souls of all fine poets passed into the body of a swan. Sometimes people got that back to front; for instance, Shakespeare is commonly referred to as the Swan of Avon, presumably meaning he had the soul of a swan while he was still alive.

In Greek mythology the beautiful woman Leda was seduced by a male swan who was actually Jupiter in disguise and she laid eggs which resulted in four children, one of whom was the beautiful Helen of Troy.

Among these many fascinations with the swan there grew intrigue that, unlike most other birds, the swan does not sing. (One kind, the whistling swan, makes a marginally musical sound.) So someone came up with the weird belief that swans *do* sing, but only once in their life, most beautifully, just before they're about to die. Whoever that someone was, it was a long time ago because Plato was talking about it 300 years before the birth of Jesus. And a lot of other very eminent people talked about it too: Cicero, Seneca, Euripides, Aristotle, etc. Some of them denied that it was true, but the legend continued to take hold. Poet Edmund Spenser referred to it in the 16th century, and Shakespeare referred to it in *Othello* early in the 17th century. The line between myth and legend was well and truly crossed — many people believed then, and somehow believe now, that a swan will sing only once, just before it dies.

In more recent times, the term has taken on a slightly different meaning, namely that someone is doing something for the last time — even if they have been quite good at it for years. We now use swansong not about someone whose life is coming to an end, but whose effective working days are numbered, and their swansong could be their last great effort.

The last word on this matter goes to poet Samuel Taylor Coleridge, in 1809, who wrote:

Swans sing before they die — 'twere no bad thing
Did certain persons die before they sing.

 Was *Sweet Fanny Adams* ever a real person?

Yes there was a real Sweet Fanny Adams, but the connection with the expression is horrible.

Fanny Adams was a little eight-year-old girl in Hampshire in England. In 1867 she was found brutally murdered in a hop field, with her body hideously dismembered and spread all over the place. The case was widely publicised (just as such cases are today) and everyone knew who sweet Fanny Adams was.

Round about the same time, the navy introduced a new kind of food on ships: tinned mutton. Rather callously, the sailors referred to this messy food as Sweet Fanny Adams because of its similarity to unidentifiable body parts. The use of the term became quite common and eventually came to mean something worthless or, later, nothing at all.

Then, during the 20th century, military troops further corrupted the image because of the similarity of initials with another vernacular phrase, fuck all. There was no connection between the two expressions; they just happened to have the same initials.

This expression gradually became reduced to initials, sweet FA or just SFA, which at least had the advantage of removing poor little Fanny Adams from the image.

 What is the origin and meaning of the expression *Sydney or the bush*?

The use is Australian, but fairly straightforward, if you accept that the bush means anywhere distant from the mainstream, the mainstream in this case being Sydney.

The expression has been used since the late 19th century in Australia, meaning that you have to make a choice about something — will you choose Sydney or the bush? *An Economic History of Australia* uses the expression, explaining that it is something most Australians say when they're gambling with a decision.

Q How is the word *tack* used in connection with land?

The word tack has a very old meaning in Scotland and parts of north England. It is used in three different ways, and they're all to do with land which is leased or rented:
(1) The money paid for the leasing of land can be called the tack.
(2) The land being leased is sometimes called tack land.
(3) The period of time for which the land is leased can be referred to as a tack of . . . weeks, years.
The basic meaning of the word is agreement made or bargain struck.

Q Where does the word *tad* come from?

It originates in the United States and started out as meaning something small (as it still does) but originally, in full, the word was tadpole, which is small — in comparison with, say, us. Over time, tadpole became shorted to tad and no longer refers just to a small creature, but to a small amount of anything. 'Do you have milk in your tea?' 'Yes, but just a tad.'

Q Why is the Edinburgh *Tattoo* so called?

It has nothing to do with the word tattoo meaning a design engraved on the body; that is a Tahitian word which Captain Cook came across in the 18th century and brought back to England where it has become the accepted word, in any context at all — not just

Polynesian — for a design put into the skin with indelible dyes.

The military word tattoo has been in the English language a whole 100 years longer, and although it is pronounced and written the same way, it has an entirely different meaning and different ancestry. A military tattoo is the signal that it is time for soldiers to return to their barracks — the music of drums and fifes tells them their leave is up. This ritual and its music have eventually evolved into a large military ceremony called a tattoo.

During the 17th century, the drums and fifes went out into the villages to play the music that recalled the soldiers, and the military men would fall in and march behind them. Naturally the villagers gathered to watch. When this happened in Holland, the innkeepers would call out tap toe, which roughly means close down the barrels — the beer stopped flowing and no grog was sold while the troops marched out of town. In time, the ancient Dutch phrase filtered across to England (which is not many kilometres away) and gradually became pronounced as tattoo, and the instruction to stop selling grog became the name of the military ceremony itself.

 Q **Where does the saying *teach your grandmother to suck eggs* come from?**

The ancestor of the expression is in the works of the Dutch scholar Erasmus in the 1500s. The expression was translated into English but over the centuries it has gone through various forms: teach an old dame to spin, teach your grandmother to grope ducks, or the version that probably led to eggs, teach your grandmother to sup sour milk. It had certainly become eggs by 1749 when it appeared in Henry Fielding's famous novel *Tom Jones*.

The expression is intended to mean don't tell someone how to do something they already know how to do.

Why does the Lord's prayer have the words 'Lead us not into _temptation_'. This implies that the Lord intends to lead us into temptation, and is asked not to?

It is the problem of translation. The Lord's Prayer has its basis in ancient Jewish prayers and scholars believe Jesus would have been familiar with the Hebrew versions. Jesus is reported to have taught his version to his disciples and the text that later became familiar to English speakers came through biblical Aramaic and Greek before it came into English.

There have been difficulties with the translations all along, for instance with the word bread: the word originally used was one that might not have meant what we call bread at all. A number of scholars have studied the texts and made various alterations over several hundred years.

In the mid-1970s an inter-denominational Christian group called the International Consultation on English Texts proposed some preferred reassignments in the English text of the Lord's Prayer which had been in use for some time. One of the lines they had concern about was 'Lead us not into temptation', which is an inverted negative with ellipsis in the second person imperative case — in other words, in full modern English it seems to be saying Do not lead us into temptation, and thus clearly suggests that the Lord might.

The Anglican church accepted the proposal of a slightly different translation in 1977 and the Roman Catholic church has also made a slight variation along the suggested lines, so nowadays it seems to be generally agreed among the major Christian groups that it is acceptable to say: 'Do not bring us to the time of trial' or 'Save us from the time of trial'. And that, it is to be hoped, negates the impression that the English version of the Jesus version of the ancient Hebrew prayers gives . . . that the Lord would deliberately tempt people.

Is it true that the words *testimony*, *testimonial* and *testify* are related to the word *testicle*?

The short answer is yes, they all mean the same thing: some form of witness. *Testis* is the Latin word for witness, meaning making a statement, and various grammatical forms of the word mean various related things: *testificari* survives as testimony, the giving of information sworn to be true, and *testicularis* survives in English as testicle, which was seen by the ancient Romans as being witness to, or a statement of, virility and masculinity.

There is reason to believe that in some ancient civilisations, when young men applied to graduate into full citizenship, they were obliged to give testimony to the city council that they were adult, which actually meant showing their testicles in order to prove that they were fully grown and were not eunuchs or women in disguise. So in the original Latin giving testimony actually means showing the testicles and allowing them to be examined.

 Did the 1878 Gilbert and Sullivan opera *HMS Pinafore* invent the phrase *give three cheers and one cheer more*?

W.S. Gilbert did not invent it. You hear it quite often in that opera — 'Give three cheers and one cheer more, for the well-bred captain of the *Pinafore*' — because it makes a convenient rhyme. And it's somewhat deceiving: because a naval captain in that opera is cheered, we think it's a naval custom.

But in fact the research library of the Royal Navy says that there is no record of it being a specifically naval custom; it crops up in various places to indicate a very special occasion, sometimes involving the Navy, sometimes not.

The custom of giving three cheers plus one cheer more goes much further back than Gilbert and Sullivan; there are records of it being a yacht club ritual well over 100 years before when, say, an admiral and a captain were at the same ceremony and three cheers would be given for the admiral, who acknowledged this, and then one cheer more for the captain. And the pattern is sometimes followed when ships pass each other at sea — each ship gives three long toots on the whistle, followed by one short toot.

You'll also find the practice in the history of New Zealand. I believe the proclamation that established Auckland included a ceremony wherein three cheers were given, and then one cheer more. And that also was well before Gilbert and Sullivan.

You'll find it in Chapter 13 of Dickens's *Pickwick Papers* where it occurs as a special amplification of a joyous occasion — and that was 41 years before *HMS Pinafore*. Dickens, like Gilbert, uses it in a rather comic, non-military way.

 How did *the three wise monkeys* come to represent the catchphrase 'see no evil, hear no evil, speak no evil'?

The concept of three wise creatures who see no evil, hear no evil and speak no evil *may* have existed in China possibly as far back as the 5th century BC, long before it became popular in Japan. So the basic idea could have been around for over 2000 years, reminding us that evil is a matter of choice.

But the actual image we have in modern times, of three monkeys shielding their eyes, lips and ears from evil, definitely originates in 17th-century Japan. The earliest known depiction of the celebrated trio is to be found on the walls of the magnificent Toshogu shrine in the little town of Nikko, and it's still there — on the walls of the stable that housed the temple's sacred horses. Why on the stable walls? Japanese people believe that monkeys are always friends to horses, keeping them free from illness and providing them with amiable company.

The Toshogu shrine was finished in 1636, and the popularity of the picture of three wise monkeys gradually spread throughout the world. By the end of the 19th century they had become an established image in Western decor.

But since monkeys are more famous for being mischievous and full of devilry, why then does the old legend describe these three as wise? The Japanese say that it is a trick of the language. The motto 'See no evil, hear no evil, speak no evil' has existed in Japan for hundreds of years. But the Japanese language has a certain way of making a verb negative: they add the word *zaru*, and when this is added to a word like run you end up with the equivalent of run-not. In the famous monkey motto it is see-not etc. The Japanese word for monkey is *saru*, so some scholars believe that, over the centuries of saying the motto, the word *zaru* became associated in people's minds with the word *saru* in the motto. Hence, in time, the instruction 'See not evil' took on the added meaning that monkeys exemplified the saying. And that had happened by the time the famous carving was done in 1636.

By now literally hundreds of thousands of versions of the three wise monkeys exist, in every conceivable substance: miniatures made in gold and set with jewels, shelf-size in brass right up to life-size wise monkeys of concrete for garden decoration. They can be found made of porcelain, alabaster, plaster of Paris, wood, bronze, nickel and pewter. They adorn door knockers, cigarette boxes, bookends, paperweights, wine bottles and toasting forks. The three wise monkeys are everywhere.

 Why are we sometimes *thrilled to bits*?

It's an old expression in English, sometimes heard in such variations as to fall to bits, where to bits means completely apart.

This word bit comes from the Old English word *bite*, meaning a piece small enough to be torn off with the teeth. So, to be completely pedantic, the expression once meant to be so thrilled that one had fallen apart into little bites.

How did the expression *throw the book at* come about?

It originates in the court of law — well, if not *in* the court, then about the court. The expression isn't all that old; it is believed to have first appeared in print in 1932 and in those days it still had connotations of actual law. The book was the register of all acts deemed to be criminal and the punishments for them, so to say throw the book at someone meant to file all criminal charges that were possible in a particular circumstance.

Nowadays it has broadened a bit: it still means that a set of regulations will be invoked, but not necessarily criminal charges.

 A person who is willing to do something, often says they will *throw their hat in the ring*. Why?

In the days when boxing matches were rather less organised than they are now, pre-David Tua and global telecasts, a freelance boxer would stand in the ring and issue a challenge. Then whoever was inclined to accept the challenge threw their hat into the ring.

The phrase seems to have come into the language about 1820, meaning to put yourself forward for a job or a responsibility. When he was running for president in 1912, Theodore Roosevelt used the expression publicly: 'My hat's in the ring, the fight is on and I'm stripped to the buff'.

 Can any actual date be assigned when you hear the expression *time immemorial*?

There used to be a definite date, but nowadays people don't usually have an exact date in mind when they say time immemorial.

It was originally a legal term, defined in British law by a statute of Westminster in the year 1275. The statute decided to fix a time limit for the bringing of certain legal actions, and that time limit was to be the reign of King Richard I. Anything that happened before then was said to have happened beyond legal memory or in time immemorial. Richard I became king in 1189 so for many decades the strict meaning of the phrase time immemorial was anything before 1189. If you wanted to bring a legal action about something, it had to be something that had happened after that date.

Over the centuries, the legal aspect has faded away and the meaning has doubled so that when people say since time immemorial they mean that something has been in existence for a very long time. And when they say until time immemorial they mean way into the future.

Q Where does the phrase *a tinker's damn* come from?

There has been some confusion here between dam, meaning a structure that holds something back, and damn, meaning a curse. In this context it is dam: old-time tinkers (metalworkers) used a ball of bread dough to plug a hole while they soldered it from the other side; they created a miniature dam. When the soldering was complete the dam was useless, so not worth a tinker's dam came to mean worthless.

Confusion over dam/damn led to a drift towards saying 'not worth a tinker's curse', but the original dam was not a swear word but a throwaway piece of bread.

Q What is the origin of the expression *a tissue of lies*?

The word tissue comes from Latin *texere*, meaning *to weave*. In earlier times it has been used to describe thick luxurious fabrics, though nowadays it has evolved more towards a thin, delicate fabric, or even a thin substance that isn't actually woven at all, like tissue paper.

But the earlier image of weaving survives in the expression tissue of lies, in which tissue means a woven fabric intertwining several different threads. The implication is that one falsehood invariably leads to another and a web of deception results.

How did the expression *tit for tat* begin?

A form of this expression, meaning retaliation, has been used in English for centuries. Before the 16th century people said tip for tap, possibly derived from Dutch *dis vor dat* meaning this for that, which itself derives from Latin *quid pro quo*. After the mid-1500s the expression subtly changed to tit for tat, and became part of Cockney rhyming slang: titfer (tit for tat), meaning hat.

Some questions about *titles*.

 If a man and woman are married, but the wife does not use the husband's surname, what happens if the husband is made a knight?

There is no legal requirement for a married woman to use her husband's surname; it is only a social custom. Mr John Smith can quite legally be married to Ms Joan Wilson.

But if Mr John Smith becomes Sir John Smith, his wife has a choice. She can quite correctly choose to be called Lady Smith, if she decides to use her husband's surname. But if she is consistently known as Ms Wilson, then she can't change from Ms to Lady and become Lady Wilson. She shares her husband's title only if she shares his surname. (Remember, too, that a woman has to be a duke's daughter or an earl's daughter to have the word lady in front of her *first* name.)

 If a titled man and his wife divorce, the divorced wife still retains a *title* as long as she still carries her ex-husband's surname. If the titled man then marries someone else, would there be two women with the same title?

The short answer is yes. This isn't uncommon. Divorcing does not automatically remove the surname from the divorced party.

So as long as she retains the surname, she retains the title. And the new wife would automatically share her husband's title, so it's quite possible there would be two people called Lady Smith.

This can happen at quite a high level — there once were two Duchesses of Westminster, and two Duchesses of Marlborough.

Q **Does a dame's husband get to be called any *title*?**

The short answer is no: if a man has a title he always shares it with his legal wife, but if a woman has a title, she never shares it with her legal husband.

This applies even to the Queen. Her father was a real king, and he shared the title with his wife, who was called Queen Elizabeth, and addressed as Your Majesty. But Prince Philip is not called King, and is not addressed as Your Majesty. (She bestowed the title of prince upon him.)

A woman with her own title can change her surname many times, but she still keeps the title on her first name. For example, Dame Zara Holt remarried and became Dame Zara Bates, and Princess Anne has had two husbands, but she still remains Princess Anne. Diana, on the other hand, was only a princess by marriage: the title was attached to her surname, Windsor. She never was Princess Diana, only Princess of Wales.

Q **Why are *toadstools* so called?**

Quite simply, toadstools are little stools for toads to sit on, but the word has a strange history. What we call toadstools used to be called paddock stools, about 500 years ago, when the word paddock used to mean a toad (1398).

In those days, a paddock, a field with some sort of boundary, was called a parrock. That word survives in English as our ordinary word park. But the field somehow took over the word for toad, then people started to say paddock meaning a field, not a toad. To replace it, the word toad came into use instead of paddock and toadstool took over from the earlier paddock stool. Paddock and puddock are still used in parts of Britain to describe a toad.

 Why we do *toast* people and how did the word come about? Is there a connection with the toast we have for breakfast?

The custom of taking a sip of drink to salute someone originates in ancient Greece, in the 6th century BC when political poisoning was not unknown, especially in decanters of wine. To demonstrate integrity to guests, a host would always sip the first wine poured from the decanter, and the others then knew it was safe to follow suit. This gradually developed into a practice of acknowledging the first drink taken as a sign of friendship or acknowledgement.

The ancient Romans developed a new twist: they added a piece of burnt bread to glasses of wine. Winemaking wasn't so sophisticated in those days and it was believed that a tiny quantity of charcoal actually reduced the acidity in wines. The Latin for parched or roasted is *tostus*, hence our word toast.

Over hundreds of years, the two customs blended into one word: the Greek custom of drinking to salute a person, and the Roman habit of dunking a piece of toast into wine.

Q **Where does *togs*, as in swimming togs, come from?**

This is faintly surprising, because togs, in contemporary English, is descended directly from the ancient Roman word *toga*, which itself comes from a Latin word *tegere*, meaning to cover. The word has migrated into English to mean clothes — usually as a verb, as in all togged up, meaning wearing full and elaborate clothing.

But the short noun togs, which survives mainly to describe swimwear, is, simply, a modern version of toga.

He tells more lies than *Tom Pepper*. Who was Tom Pepper?

Tom Pepper doesn't actually exist, and never did. The expression is an old nautical saying that refers to a mythical character whom sailors used to say was kicked out of hell because he told so many lies. This piece of folklore has been around since the middle of the 19th century, but isn't often heard so you can assume that anyone who says it probably has a nautical background or had a father or grandfather who did.

The expression doesn't really make sense. One would think that telling lies was a recommendation for staying in hell but, according to legend, Tom Pepper was thrown out.

 Why does someone *go to the ton* when they do 100 mph?

A real ton used to be a common measure of weight and for some unknown reason it became a slang expression meaning 100. The most common use of this expression was in motor-bike racing, where doing a ton meant going at 100 mph, which was considered an ultimate test for both the machine and the rider. This gave rise to a slang description of young people who rode motor bikes too fast in general: they were called ton-up kids.

The term ton is also used in darts and cricket to indicate 100, and in underworld slang it used to mean £100.

 Whatever is the origin of '*Too late,*' she cried, and waved her wooden leg?

It seems to be a combination of two different phrases which have somehow become joined up.

Early in the 20th century the military originated a sort of joke about a man who fell into a part of the sea that was full of sharks. He called for help but before assistance could reach him the sharks began to attack so that when help did arrive, he had to call out, 'Too late, too late'. By now, however, the sharks had damaged him below water, and he called out in a very high voice. You sometimes still hear that phrase just on its own, said in a funny falsetto voice.

Then after the First World War girls started going to public dances unchaperoned, just turning up at such events in groups. If a fellow was clumsy or for some reason not a desirable person to dance with, the word would go round very quickly, and a catchphrase developed that when a man asked a girl to dance and she didn't want to, instead of just saying *no*, she would say, 'I'm sorry, but I've got a wooden leg.' Somehow, the two phrases came together, and a new version developed: 'Too late', she cried, and waved her wooden leg.

 Why do people say *touch wood* and exactly what do they mean?

This goes way back to early primitive times when it was believed that a lot of objects in nature had supernatural powers, and spirits that lived in them. Many trees were believed to have sacred significance and some in particular were thought to possess the power of protection, e.g. the oak, the ash, the hazel and the willow. So, in order to make sure something good happened, and to avert bad luck, people would appeal to one of these trees and the spirits in them, or better still, hug the tree.

Over centuries, the actual focus on specific trees for specific things has faded away, and the hugging has been reduced but its remnant remains very firmly in our culture, because people quite often say touch wood (knock on wood in the United States) when they want to avert something bad, and they always touch wood when they say it. (Sometimes in this age of plastics and formica, you see people desperately look around the room for something which really is wood.)

There is also a connection with touching the cross on which Jesus died: touching wood somehow symbolised your connection with this icon, thus showing your own willingness to be a good person, and bringing good things to you. But the concept of trees having a spirit is much older and was firmly believed long before Jesus was born. This is another example of Christianity attaching a significance to an existing belief.

 Where does the word *Trafalgar* actually come from?

It isn't an English word. All the places in London named for it commemorate the Battle of Trafalgar, which took place on the south coast of Spain at Trafalgar in 1805.

Its name and the exact Arabic derivation are lost in antiquity. There are two schools of thought about the Arabic origin. In Arabic, *tarf* means sand or earth and *el garb* means the west, so a sandy point to the west could be *tar-el-garb*. But that particular cape is also believed to be possibly the home of one of the legendary pillars of Hercules, in which case the name might have been *taraf-al-aghar*, the pillar from the cave.

 The word *tripe* is used to express disgust or to mean useless talk. How did this expression come about?

The connection between actual tripe, and something you want to describe as off-putting, is fairly obvious. The word tripe has been in the English language for over 600 years, meaning the lining of an animal's stomach cavity — and if you see it in its raw state it is distinctly unattractive. Even after it has been cleaned and dressed it is still not entirely pleasant.

The eating of tripe may well have arisen among people of what are called 'the lower socio-economic levels' where every part of a beast was used up because they couldn't afford to waste anything. Nowadays the world is fairly clearly divided into those who can't stand the thought or sight of tripe, and those who really like it: there is a Tripe and Onions Club that meets and invents different ways of cooking and serving tripe.

Describing something you don't agree with as tripe isn't a very old expression. Cricketers have used the expression since about 1920 to mean easy bowling, and they seem to have borrowed that from the military, who've been using the word for about 100 years to describe anything dirty — probably because tripe in its raw state *is* very dirty indeed. And they would also say that if someone was in trouble, they were in tripe — being surrounded by tripe would undoubtedly be an unpleasant situation.

Round about the same time, tripe became attached to the word hound, and a tripe-hound was a low, disgusting fellow. Fairly early in the 20th century this expression was transferred to newspaper reporters. Gradually, the term moved away from journalists to sheep dogs, and then to just any old dog at all.

But there could be a significance in the fact that it was a slang term meaning newspaper reporters because, by a slight shift of perception, it could mean *not* that they wrote material which was dirty and filthy, but that a lot of what was written and reported was useless and boring. Hence, a badly written book would be sheer tripe, a speech could be all tripe and so on.

 In New Zealand's national anthem what do the words 'Guard Pacific's *triple star*' actually refer to?

Nobody knows the full truth about this. New Zealand used to be divided into three main provinces — New Ulster (North Island), New Munster (South Island) and New Leinster (Stewart Island) — but they were abandoned in 1852, over 20 years before the song was written, so it can't have meant that.

Could it have meant three islands? That seems remotely possible, but New Zealand has dozens of islands and some of them, such as Kapiti, figured more prominently in the country's history than Stewart Island. So we simply don't know if Thomas Bracken meant three islands.

The constellation of stars known as the Southern Cross has four stars, so he can't have meant that.

One of the most tortuous explanations is that by triple Bracken actually meant truple, short for quadruple, thus four stars, but, there is absolutely no evidence for that at all.

Another theory is that he intended to write 'Guard Pacific's triple shore' and wrote star by mistake but there is no evidence for that either — and the only reason it was suggested in the first place is that shore would have rhymed with war whereas star doesn't. But Bracken supervised the poem through several print forms, in magazine, book and sheet music, so he can't possibly have allowed star instead of shore on about 10 occasions, and it doesn't make sense anyway.

The only possibly relevant fact anyone can come up with is that the Anglican Bishop Selwyn's diocesan coat of arms featured three stars. (It still does: you can see those three stars in places like the insignia of the Diocescan Anglican school for girls in Auckland.) Bracken was born into a Protestant family in County Meath in Ireland, he later (in 1896) became a Roman Catholic. Bishop Selwyn's insignia may have been recognisable in Dunedin and it is possible that, since Bracken was still a Protestant in 1876, when the words were written, he was exalting the bishop.

So there are several different explanations as to what 'Pacific's triple star' *might* have meant and they all contradict each other. Each of them is feasible, ardently believed by its own school of thought but not able to be proved.

Q **What is the origin of the word *trollop*?**

There is a difference between Trollope, with an e on the end, and trollop without an e. The first is a family name, still extant and believed to have been derived from an ancestor who was an eminent hunter nicknamed 'Trois Lupes' (three wolves). The second has two possible sources.

(1) The German word *trollen* means to wander, and two common English words are descended from it: stroll (meaning to amble about) and trolley (which rumbles along but has no driving force).

Now that German word may also have become shortened in English to troll, which is now a real English word with two separate meanings: to draw a fishing line through the water or to wander the streets, possibly looking for sexual adventure. There's an obvious similarity between that second meaning of troll and trollop, but they're not necessarily from the same source.

(2) There was also once a very old German dialect word *trull* which meant a prostitute. That German word also migrated into English in the 1600s, and somehow changed its spelling to become troll. This was often used to describe something hanging loosely, like baggy clothes. This word, describing a woman whose clothes were ill-fitting and haphazard, *may* have extended into meaning the woman was also loose herself, so trull became troll then became trollop. Nobody is sure.

And there's also one other confusing factor. The Scandinavian word *troll* is quite well known in English — a supernatural creature who lives in a cave. So if someone shortens trollop to just troll, people could think the woman they're referring to is ugly, misshapen and lives in a cave.

The male equivalents of trollop are: rake, roué, libertine, lecher, Don Juan, Romeo, philanderer, lady-killer, seducer, Lothario, bed-hopper and the current favourite, a stud.

 Q **Is *trug*, the name of a flat gardening basket with little feet, connected to truck?**

The word trug has had two meanings in English: it is the rather pleasant name for a flat gardening basket but in the 17th century it was also the slang word for prostitute, and the terms trugging or trug-house weren't used in polite society. Gardeners will be pleased that this meaning has vanished.

But according to scholars the English word trug is closely related to the old German word *Trog*, which also gives us the English word trough.

The word truck is not related to the word trough at all. Trough is Old German and truck comes from old Anglo-Norman, originally Latin *trochlea*. The modern word truck is the shortened version of truckle.

There are many meanings for the words truck and truckle but they nearly always have something to do with movement: bits of boats are called trucks, theatre and TV scenery built on platforms with wheels are known as trucks and beds that can be rolled are called truckle beds.

There is an entirely different word, the verb to truck, meaning to barter and have business dealings. It probably comes from the Latin *trocare* and you still hear it in use: 'I will have no truck with him', meaning I won't have any association or business dealings with him.

But another very old meaning of truck is little bits and pieces, especially garden produce. A 19th-century advertisement referred to gardeners having a truck basket, into which you put bits and pieces of things you need when gardening, plus the fruits and vegetables you were picking. That is distinctly an old meaning of truck.

It is coincidence that the basket they described is also called a trug basket, they are two different words. In general, anything that sounds like truck is to do with movement, and trough generally means something that stands still.

 Are *tulips* so called because it is short for two lips?

No. They are called tulips because of the way they are shaped, but it has nothing to do with lips.

Tulips originate in Turkey — thousands are grown in Holland but the plant definitely comes originally from Turkey — and their name is a Turkish word *tulben*, meaning turban, because of the way that tulip petals sit: they look a bit like a wrapped turban.

 Does the expression *turn over a new leaf* refer to the pages of a book or the spring growth on a tree?

It means to make a fresh start and mend your ways. In Oscar Wilde's *The Importance of Being Earnest* Miss Prism suggests someone turn over a new leaf, and his reply is that he has already begun a whole volume. That suggests that Wilde thought it meant the leaf of a book rather than the leaf of a tree.

And Wilde was right. Probably the earliest printing of the expression is in *Holinshed's Chronicles of England, Scotland and Ireland*, published in 1577, which says 'he must turn the leaf and take out a new lesson' — and that indicates a book, not a tree.

Q What is the explanation for the word *turncoat*?

Turncoat has a fairly simple meaning: a person who deserts one cause and applies themselves to another. They deny what they said they believed in before, and embrace something different, usually the opposition.

There is a fairly standard belief that in long-ago Germany, the powerful Duke of Saxony had lands on the border between Germany and France. This inevitably involved negotiations of some sort or another between French and German interests, and the duke thought of having a coat or cloak made up which was blue on one side and white on the other.

When he wanted to show that he was acting in the interests of France he wore the white side of the coat on the outside, and when he wanted the Saxon Germans to have faith in him, he wore the blue side out. So the Duke of Saxony is believed to have been the original turncoat. But he was acting in the interests of harmonious politics, rather than betrayal.

The word stayed on, but gradually the meaning evolved into something slightly different: fighting men who deserted one army for another could also change the colours they showed in battle by turning their coat or tabard inside out. So now the word is firmly associated with a person who deliberately deserts his principles and takes on a different colour.

Q What is the background to the *two-fingered salute*?

This ancient and well-known gesture of sticking two fingers in the air has quite a different origin from what is usually called giving the finger, which is just one finger stuck in the air — though both are gestures of derision and insult.

It is generally accepted that the two-fingered salute originated with military bowmen over 500 years ago. Before battles, there was a formal pronouncement by heralds that bowmen captured by the enemy would have the precious first two fingers on their right hand cut off. The opposing side would often belligerently stick up their two fingers, to show that they were still whole and healthy and intended to remain so — and they shouted insults while they did it. Gradually, this became a general gesture of defiance, with the backs of the fingers facing outwards.

Several centuries later, Sir Winston Churchill created history by turning his hand round the other way and turning the traditional gesture into a V-for-Victory sign. It is reported that sometimes, when he was with the troops and there were no cameras present, he would deliberately reverse his hand and make the old-fashioned insulting gesture, while looking up at the sky where the Germans were expected. The troops enjoyed that enormously.

The one-finger salute, believed to be of American origin, is much more recent and rather more anatomical. Sometimes described as the check-your-oil gesture, it is always done with the hand facing inwards and the *middle* finger lifted and facing outwards. It refers to a crude and painful bodily exploration.

Q | During the Princess of Wales's funeral, the flag flying above Buckingham Palace was referred to as the *Union*, not the *Union Jack*. Why?

Flag terminology is immensely complex.

There are 19 different meanings for the word jack and one of them is that, in nautical terms, a jack is the small flag that flies at the bow of a ship to show its nationality. Now when Britain's official flag settled down in 1801, its exact design and colouring were meticulously written out by order of council, which described it as 'the Union Flag'. That order still stands today, so although in everyday speech people will say Union Jack, most of the time it isn't correct to say jack at all, one reason being that it might not be on a ship at the time.

And when it's above Buckingham Palace and being referred to by BBC commentators or British journalists, it would be called by its correct formal name, which is the Union flag, or just the Union.

 Q | Why is nothing over *until the fat lady sings*?

This expression is recent: it's believed to have been first said in 1978. In that year, American sports writer Dan Cook attended a rodeo with another journalist friend. At one point the other man remarked, 'The rodeo ain't over until the bull riders ride' and Mr Cook replied by saying, 'And the opera ain't over until the fat lady sings.' Cook's remark was published in the *Washington Post* on 18 June 1978 and very quickly went into common parlance. One assumes that, in 1978, opera stars were fatter than they are now.

Two years later, in 1980, the Oxford University Press acknowledged it as a popular phrase, and it became even more common during periods of stock market crisis.

Nowadays the expression has evolved into the *show* isn't over until the fat lady sings and means something like the main action of the event hasn't happened yet and everyone uses it in many different contexts.

 When something has gone wrong, why do we say it is *up the shoot*?

Up the shoot derives from up the spout, an old word for pawnbroker (sometimes just called a spout). When something was pawned, the broker put his docket into a spout, sometimes called a shoot. So being up the spout or up the shoot came to mean short of money, even bankrupt. Then it expanded to include being sick, in hospital or in prison, and now it means flawed in some way.

What does St *Valentine* have to do with chocolates and expensive roses?

Absolutely nothing. There was a real Valentine; in fact there were two, and it's not quite clear which was which, but the feast day of St Valentine was established as 14 February a very long time ago.

Some very thin myths and well-cultivated legends have tried to encourage a connection between Valentine and lovers, but there is no guarantee at all about the truth of any of the stories, and since both the original gentlemen were Roman Catholic priests they had no experience of romance or marriage.

The truth about the connection with lovers, if there is one, seems to be more in the date, mid-February being the time of year in the northern hemisphere when birds start to mate. Birds must be fairly public about this, because their mating rituals and the time they did them, are widely established. Even Chaucer mentioned it in his *Parliament of Fowls*:

> For this was on Saint Valentines Day,
> When every bird cometh here to choose his match.

So it's not difficult to see that the two ideas of mating, and St Valentine, gradually came together.

This has been wildly encouraged by the merchants and marketers so nowadays we are exhorted to buy thousands of products that have nothing whatever to do with St Valentine or birds, all through a somewhat tenuous connection with mating. The encouragement of the legend is really all about spending money.

Q **Where does the expression** *vent one's spleen* **come from?**

It's fairly straightforward. The spleen, in olden times, was thought to be the organ that governed the emotions, especially melancholy. Gradually the word spleen came to mean negative emotions such as spitefulness and bad temper.

Vent, derived originally from the Latin word for wind, means a small opening, or to release something through a small opening, usually suddenly. Thus, venting one's spleen meant creating an opportunity to unleash all the bad thoughts you were harbouring, usually in a rush.

Walla-walla-cat's-meat-eat-brown-bread
— where does it come from?

This was a popular vernacular saying in Britain during the 1940s. Every decade has fashionable nonsense phrases — some last and some don't. In ye olden times there was O waly waly, and hey nonny no, and some people still say things like nanu nanu (a survivor from the TV show *Mork and Mindy*) or yabba dabba doo, as Fred Flintstone did. They become sound pictures that have a fragile and transient life, and their meaning usually adapts to the context in which they're said. But, as with all pictures, some stay on the wall and some disappear into the cupboard, and I think walla-walla-cat's-meat-eat-brown-bread has nowadays gone into the cupboard.

But the explanation for this strange expression is rather unfortunate. Shortly after the Second World War, Britain began to have a number of immigrants who were dark-skinned. This didn't go down particularly well with some of the locals, and this phrase originated as a sort of taunt or put down. Walla-walla — imitating the supposed sound of jungle rituals; cat's-meat — because many of the immigrants were so poor they subsisted on meat the British would only keep for cats; and eat brown bread — a rhyming substitute for dead. So, broken down like that, the phrase meant darkies drop dead.

Q **Where does the expression *warm fuzzies* come from?**

The expression appears to have been first published in the 1970s by American educationalist author Thomas Gordon in *Teacher*

Effectiveness Training, a guidebook for teachers of 6–12-year-olds. Warm fuzzies acknowledges that something has been well done, *or* the reaction from knowing something has been well done. Of course, Thomas Gordon may have been quoting someone else.

From the same book comes the opposite, cold pricklies — a put-down, a snide acknowledgement or the reaction from someone's being snide. One of the two expressions caught on, but the other didn't.

Q What is the origin of the expression *weasel words*?

These are words that detract from or weaken the effectiveness or force of another expression. This term first appeared in print in 1900 written by Stewart Chaplin in *Century Magazine*. The article — 'The Stained Glass Political Platform' — referred to the phrase 'duly protected' as weasel words. But the phrase became much more famous when Theodore Roosevelt used it in a speech in 1916 — he said 'when a weasel sucks eggs the meat is sucked out. If you use a weasel word there is nothing left of the other.'

There are some wonderful comments about weasel words in Joe Bennett's book of columns *Sleeping Dogs and Other Lies*. He points out that both 'streamlining their operations in response to market forces' and 'restructuring' mean, quite simply, that people are going to be sacked. Similarly he explains that a 'strategic plan to modify core business' means they're going to start doing something different from what we've all become accustomed to them doing.

 Q *What goes round comes round* seems to mean that if there are rumours about you, sooner or later you'll have to face up to them. Is this right?

Language scholars seem to think this possibly started out as a version of the English expression what goes up must come down.

That fits with the way the expression was first used — things will happen as they will; fate or kismet will dictate circumstances, whatever we say or do.

It has been used in this way in the United States. It had appeared in print there in 1969 by the American writer Donald Goines who served seven gaol sentences before he began to write and so possibly had an insight into what could be called grassroots philosophy.

But the expression seems to have changed a bit in that nowadays there's a connotation that if you start a piece of slander about someone, eventually you will be identified as the bad-mouther, or if you do something underhand or illegal, eventually you'll be found out.

 Q **'From whoa to go' seems to be a reversal of the usual expression. How did that come about?**

Whoa is an old English word, used to stop horses — it's a variation on ho, which is just a yelling out word to attract attention — as in land ho!

Go to whoa has been in use in Australasia since 1950, and is simply a slightly colourful way of saying from start to finish, or to be moving and come to a stop, or having run its full course.

So somewhere within those 50 years, some smart person has started using it back to front, whoa to go, which seems to mean that which was at rest has started to move, something or someone has been activated.

This sort of language development happens all the time and I don't think there's anything that can be done about it: there's no copyright on linguistic evolvement.

 Q **What is the origin of the expression *the whole nine yards*?**

Its meaning is fairly clear — to go the full monty, go the whole hog, go over the top, the lot — but unfortunately its origin is very much open to question. There are four explanations, each passionately believed by four groups of people.

(1) One source says that it comes from American gridiron football where a run of 9 yards gained major credits.

(2) Several other research sources say it comes from American concreters, whose concrete mixing trucks, when full, carry 9 cubic yards — so a concreting job that uses the whole truckload means using the whole nine yards.

(3) Then there is another story, which the New Zealand Antique Arms Association agrees with, that during the Second World War American fighter pilots carried ammunition in belts 27 feet long, so if the whole belt of ammunition was used for a particularly determined attack on an enemy target, then that was using the lot — the whole nine yards!

(4) But a biochemist tells me that he has always assumed that the expression referred to the length of nucleic acid molecules in a human cell.

Q | **Where does the word *wimp* come from?**

Wimp came into the language in the 1930s in English universities, where it was applied only to girls and young women. The word travelled over to the United States where, like bimbo, it underwent a sex change and its application was slightly redefined — it was usually said about *men* who were cowardly, feeble, ineffectual.

The exact derivation of wimp is not clear but there are three schools of thought. Some scholars think it is a shortened form of whimper. Other scholars think it comes from Mr Wimpy, who was always in trouble in the Popeye cartoons.

But a third school of thought is that wimp derives from wimple, which was a soft floaty piece of fabric worn by women under the chin, from one side to another. This is not necessarily the stiff, starched wimple associated with nuns, but the original wimple worn by mediaeval ladies or movie stars like Marlene Dietrich — something silky and soft. Hence, a wimp is a person who yields to pressure easily.

 Why, when someone is scared, do they *have* or *get the wind up*?

Some understand it to be a First World War pilots' expression: if they could feel the wind coming up around their legs in those open-structured planes, they must be at stalling speed and were about to crash — and so they felt frightened.

Etymologist Eric Partridge doesn't quite concur. He agrees with the First World War pilot bit — the phrase dates to 1916 — and although he can't be definitive, his research shows that in the early days of flying, when the weather provided a fairly strong wind, it was dangerous to fly at all, which made everyone a bit nervous. Therefore when pilots said someone had the wind up, it meant that they were acting as nervously as if they had to fly a plane in a strong wind.

 Is there an etymological link between *womb* and *tomb*?

Both are enclosed dark spaces, which suggests the possibility of a connection, but they have come into English from different languages and it's just a coincidence that they both mean a cavity of some kind.

The word womb is found in Old English and it came there from the Old High German word *wamba*, meaning a hollow space, a cavity. We have to move from Old German to ancient Greek to find the other word: the Greek *tumbos* means a hill or mound, and eventually came into English as tomb.

So in fact the meanings are opposite: two enclosed spaces but one you come out of for ever, and the other one you go into for ever.

Where does *wop-wops* come from?

Out in the wop-wops means way out in some rustic area, or at least separated somehow from the mainstream. The origin is genuine Australian: wop-wops is a New Zealand abbreviation of the Australian phrase woop-woops, which itself is thought to be mock-Aboriginal. It isn't clear whether the phrase does actually exist in some Aboriginal dialect but European Australians originally started using the sound in the mid-1920s as a satirical imitation of Aboriginal words.

 Why does *working like a navvy* mean you've been working hard?

Originally the word navvy was short for navigator — not navigating at sea, but navigating the construction of canals. The canals themselves used to be known as navigations and the men who constructed them were called the navigators.

Obviously there was a great deal of heavy digging and excavating to do, and we're speaking here of a time long before the days of front-end loaders, so working like a navigator meant hard, physical work. The phrase was eventually shortened to working like a navvy and then later the expression was applied to anyone who worked hard, not just at digging canals.

 ***Wouldn't that gap your axe?* Is this a New Zealand phrase?**

It means wouldn't that annoy you and would appear to be a genuine New Zealand expression. Quite simply if you hit something accidentally and cause a notch in the cutting edge of your axe, you've ruined the axe's efficiency, which would be very annoying. The expression has extended to include any happening that holds you back and annoys you.

What is the origin of *wowser*?

It is an Australian expression, from the 19th century and means a puritanical person believing in strict limits. It is thought to derive from an old Yorkshire word, wow or wowsy, which was originally an exclamation of surprise, but came to mean a person who was always complaining, whining or being suspicious.

Y

Q **What is *yacker* and why is it always referred to as hard?**

Yacker (also yakker, yakka and yacca) is from an Aboriginal dialect word *yaga*, which simply means work. Australians began saying yacker, or hard yacker, meaning hard work, in the late 19th century, and it has been appearing in print as an acceptable informal term since 1920, though I suspect only Australasians will understand it.

Q **Why do sporting teams from South Africa often use the term *yarpie*?**

Yarpie (jarpie) is a slang term for Europeans who come from South Africa. It's not at all considered a polite term — I wouldn't say it *to* a South African.

Way back it was a variant on the name Jakobus, which looks like Jacob but can translate as James. The Afrikaans version of the name Jacob is Jaap (pronounced 'yahp') and a diminutive or affectionate version is Japie. Scholars say that it has become a contemptuous and derogatory word with a connotation of being unsophisticated and low-class.

Q **Why do we say *Your Worship* when referring to or addressing a mayor?**

This is very old — it comes from an Old English word used way back into the 12th century, *weorth*, which is the ancestor of the word worth. When it was attached to the word *scip* it became weorth-scip, meaning a vessel or container that contained or carried something valuable. Scip became the modern word ship, and in time the 'th' filtered away from weorth and we were left with worship.

Another meaning of the word developed, the verb to worship, which is rather different — to show profound religious devotion to anything considered divine. The two words have the same ancestor but slightly different meanings. As a noun, Your Worship means something of worth, such as, presumably, a mayor. As a verb, to worship means to observe religious devotion. They're not quite the same thing.

Bibliography

The following works of reference were consulted in answering the questions in this book:

Alabaster, Bikinis & Calvados: Toponymous Words, Christopher Smith
American Slang, Chapman
A.W. Reed's Place-Names of New Zealand
Biographical Dictionary of Scientists
Brewer's Dictionary of Phrase and Fable
Collins English Dictionary
Curious Facts, John May
Dictionary of Catch-phrases, Partridge
Dictionary of Clichés, Partridge
Dictionary of Eponyms, Beeching
Dictionary of Forces' Slang, Partridge
Dictionary of Slang and Unconventional English, Partridge
Dictionary of Symbolism, Biedermann
Dictionary of the Underworld, Partridge
Encyclopaedia Britannica
Extraordinary Origins of Everyday Things, Panati
Heavens to Betsy, Charles Funk
How Did It Begin?, Rudolph Brasch
In Words and Out Words, Fritz Speigel
McMillan Book of Quotations
Oxford Book of Clichés
Oxford Companion to Music
Oxford Dictionary
Oxford Dictionary of Foreign Words
Oxford Dictionary of New Words
Oxford Dictionary of New Zealand English
Place-Names of the World, Adrian Room
Popular Proverbs and Sayings, Titelman
Random House World Dictionary
The Reader's Encyclopaedia
Webster's Dictionary
Webster's Dictionary of Biography
Wordsworth Dictionary of Saints

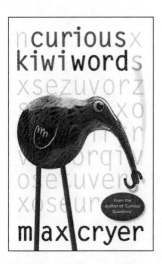

Curious Kiwi Words

New Zealanders have their own lingo — favourite words and expressions which, although not always unique to this country, have been absorbed into our lives and become part of who we are. They include words that came with the early settlers or were coined by them in response to a new environment, words that travelled across the Tasman as a result of interaction with Australia, and Maori words that came to be part of our distinctive national vocabulary.

In *Curious Kiwi Words* linguistic detective Max Cryer shares his own selection of favourite words and phrases used by New Zealanders. This is not a comprehensive dictionary, but rather a collection of those Kiwi expressions that Max considers are the most distinctive and interesting. In most cases he not only gives the meaning but also offers an illuminating potted history of the word. From 'hangi' to 'gumboots', from 'give it heaps' to 'pack a sad', *Curious Kiwi Words* is chock-full of fascinating information for Kiwis and tourists alike.

HarperCollins*Publishers*

Curious Thoughts

Best-selling author and entertainer Max Cryer returns with a
compilation of his favourite sayings, used to conclude his
'Curious Questions' slot on National Radio each Saturday
morning. From ageing disgracefully and the meaning of life,
to pithy insults and musings on the perplexing nature of the
English language, Max quips and puns his way through this
delightful selection of aphorisms . . . or should we say 'maxims'?

HarperCollins*Publishers*

Back in the Shed

What could be more quintessentially Kiwi than the shed?

Jim Hopkins and Julie Riley unearthed some wonderful characters in the best-selling *Blokes & Sheds*, and they've joined forces once more to produce a second volume devoted to New Zealand's shed culture.

Back in the Shed features the ingenuity, creativity and diversity of male and female sheddies throughout New Zealand. While the men are busy building blackcurrant harvesters, soft-rock crushers and recumbent cycles, the 'sheddettes' are getting into lead lighting, chainsaw carpentry and motorcycle maintenance. And whether it's a tangle of tools or a testament to tidiness, every shed features a treasure or two, be it an antique corn shredder, a bead-blasting cabinet or a nine-ton lathe.

From pottery to just pottering around, from tiny shacks to vast engineering emporiums, the shed is a home away from the house; *Back in the Shed* offers a unique look at this essential element of New Zealand's heartland.

HarperCollins*Publishers*

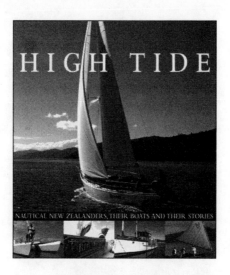

High Tide

From classic yachts to pirate ships, fishing boats to traditional waka, and luxury launches to lifeboats, the variety of boats found in New Zealand waters is astounding. New Zealanders love the ocean, and for many of us, a day on the water is close to heaven on earth. Combine this passion with a sense of adventure and a nautical bent, and you'll find the boaties featured in *High Tide* — their stories range from a boat-mad teenager who taught himself to sail aged 8 to a pair of septuagenarians learning the intricacies of fitting out an ocean cruiser. The boaties featured can be found from Kaitaia to Bluff, and everywhere in between, although they're more likely to be out on the water. The camaraderie between the guys restoring the Whanganui riverboats; the heartbreak of the Lyttelton marina disaster; the joys of cruising in the Islands; and the determination required to make a living on the water are all included in this wonderful collection of stories celebrating nautical New Zealanders.

HarperCollins*Publishers*

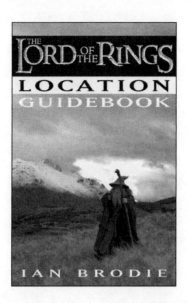

The Lord of the Rings
Location Guidebook

Since the first screening of *The Lord of the Rings: The Fellowship of the Ring* in 2001, New Zealand has become the embodiment of 'Middle-earth' to millions of moviegoers and J.R.R. Tolkien fans the world over.

This unique and definitive guidebook showcases the principle movie-set locations around New Zealand as seen in the first two films. Maps, location directions, accommodation, food and entertainment suggestions and GPS references to location sites are all provided to ensure the Middle-earth experience is as authentic as possible.

HarperCollins*Publishers*